THE URGENCY IN
Winning Souls

A Quest to Fulfill the Great Commission by
Winning the Lost at Any Cost

Pastor Dr. Claudine Benjamin

THE URGENCY IN WINNING SOULS. Copyright @ 2025. Pastor Dr. Claudine Benjamin. All rights reserved.

For more information or to book an event, contact: inspiredtowinsouls@gmail.om

No part of this publication may be reproduced, stored in a retrieval system or transmitted in any form or by any means, electronic, mechanical, photocopying, recording or otherwise without the prior written permission of the author.

Portions of this book include content adapted from The Great Commission Connection by Dr. Raymond Culpepper. Used with permission. All rights reserved.

Published by:

Editor: Cleveland O. McLeish (Author C. Orville McLeish)

ISBN: 978-1-965635-28-5 (paperback)

Unless otherwise stated, all Scripture quotations are taken from the King James Version (KJV).

Scripture quotations marked "KJV" are taken from the Holy Bible, King James Version (Public Domain).

Dedication

This book is dedicated to every believer who understands that time is short, eternity is real, and the harvest is ready.

To my children and grandchildren, I pray the burden for lost souls will rest upon you, and you will win the lost at any cost.

To the soul winners—past, present, and future—who answer the call to "go into all the world and preach the gospel," your obedience echoes in heaven.

To those burdened for the lost, may your fire never burn out. To those still waiting to step into the mission, may this book ignite a holy urgency within you.

Above all, this is dedicated to our Lord and Savior Jesus Christ—the One who came to seek and save the lost, gave us the Great Commission, and is coming again soon.

May we work while it is day, for the night is coming when no one can work.

"The fruit of the righteous is a tree of life, and he that winneth souls is wise." (Proverbs 11:30).

Acknowledgments

First and foremost, I give all glory and honor to God, whose love for humanity fuels the fire within me to fulfill the call of the Great Commission. This book would not have been possible without His divine direction, grace, and anointing.

I extend my deepest gratitude to *Dr. Raymond F. Culpepper* for his gracious permission to include selected materials from his powerful and insightful work, *The Great Commission Connection*. His lifelong commitment to evangelism and discipleship continues to inspire leaders and believers around the world. Thank you, Dr. Culpepper, for your generosity, legacy, and heart for reaching the lost.

To my family and loved ones—thank you for believing in the calling on my life and for supporting me through prayer, encouragement, and countless sacrifices. Your patience and love have carried me through many seasons, and I am forever grateful.

To my church family and those who walk alongside me in ministry, thank you for your support, encouragement, and prayers. Your love and faithfulness have strengthened me on this journey.

To every soul winner, preacher, intercessor, and disciple-maker—this book is for you. May it reignite your fire, renew your focus, and push you deeper into obedience to the Great Commission. Let us go into all the world, proclaiming the Good News and rescuing the lost, no matter the cost.

Finally, to every reader—thank you for taking this journey with me. My prayer is that this book stirs something deep within you that cannot be ignored: an urgency to win souls, a hunger to reach the unreached and a burden to fulfill the mandate of Christ in your generation.

May this book stir your heart with an unshakable urgency to win souls and become a laborer in the harvest field. I pray the words within compel you to action, deepen your compassion for the lost, and empower you to fulfill your part in the Great Commission—no matter the cost. May this book stir your heart and reignite your passion for souls with urgency, compassion, and boldness.

Together, let us win the lost at any cost.

With gratitude,

Pastor Claudine Benjamin

About the Author

Pastor Claudine Benjamin is a passionate soul-winner, a dedicated servant of the Lord, and a voice crying out in urgency to awaken the church to its divine assignment—the Great Commission. With a heart that beats for the lost and a voice that speaks truth with clarity and compassion, Pastor Claudine has spent years ministering the gospel through preaching, teaching, and personal evangelism.

Her calling is clear: to stir up a fire in believers to reach the unreached, love the unloved, and speak the truth of salvation without compromise. Drawing from scripture, personal experience, and the conviction of the Holy Spirit, she inspires others to walk boldly in their calling and become laborers in the harvest field.

Pastor Claudine is a preacher, author, mentor, and intercessor, equipping others to become bold witnesses for Christ. Her ministry carries a message of urgency, obedience, and love—reminding the church that time is short and eternity is real.

When she is not writing or ministering, she is praying, fasting, and pouring into the lives of others with unwavering commitment to the call. Her greatest desire is to hear the words, *"Well done, good and faithful servant,"* and to see multitudes come to Christ through a church that dares to answer the call.

Pastor Claudine is also a proud mother and grandmother to six beautiful grand-children.

Table of Contents

Dedication iii
Acknowledgments v
About the Author vii
Introduction: The Urgency of Winning Souls 11
Chapter 1: Everyone Can Be a Soul Winner 15
Chapter 2: The Word, Prayer, and the Holy Spirit in Soul-Winning 19
Chapter 3: Love Them Into the Kingdom 35
Chapter 4: Soul Winning in the Family 39
Chapter 5: Soul Winning in the Workplace 45
Chapter 6: How Do I Begin as a Soul Winner? 49
Chapter 7: Open-Hearted 53
Chapter 8: Ones With Difficulties 61
Chapter 9: Ones With Excuses 75
Chapter 10: The Self-Righteous Ones 81
Chapter 11: Skeptics 91
Chapter 12: Objections in Bringing Souls to Christ 105
Chapter 13: Full of Excuses 113
Chapter 14: Soul-Winning Hints 121
Chapter 15: The Uncertain 133
Chapter 16: Power for Soul-Winning 149

Chapter 17: The Indifferent 155

Chapter 18: The Great Commission 161

Chapter 19: Commanded to Preach: Biblical Preaching and the Great Commission 173

Chapter 20: Personal Evangelism and the Great Commission 189

Chapter 21: Reaching Unreached People: World Missions and the Great Commission 193

Chapter 22: Equipping the Church for Evangelism 201

Scripture Reference List: Equipping the Church for Evangelism .. 209

Scriptures on Soul Winning and the Great Commission 211

Call to Action: Your Next Steps as a Soul Winner 215

Bibliography 217

Introduction

The Urgency of Winning Souls

Soul winning is part of the Great Commission.

Jesus said in Mark 16:15, *"Go ye into all the world, and preach the gospel to every creature."* The ultimate goal, however, is to make disciples, as outlined in Matthew 28:18-20: *" And Jesus came and spake unto them, saying, All power is given unto me in heaven and in earth. Go ye therefore, and teach all nations, baptizing them in the name of the Father, and of the Son, and of the Holy Ghost: Teaching them to observe all things whatsoever I have commanded you: and, lo, I am with you always, even unto the end of the world. Amen."*

Only those who are saved can truly be disciples.

It is wise to win souls (see Proverbs 11:30).

Evangelism provides a **protective armor**: *"And your feet shod with the preparation of the gospel of peace." (Ephesians 6:15).*

Soul winning must be urgent.

The urgency comes not only from the method but from the reality of the spiritual state of mankind. Time is short, and those who die in their sins will perish in hell under the unrelenting and righteous wrath of God.

There is an urgency in winning souls because sin will cost the world dearly.

Ezekiel 18:4 says, *"Behold, all souls are mine; as the soul of the father, so also the soul of the son is mine: the soul that sinneth, it shall die."* The soul who sins will die. Souls are crying, and people are perishing. We must win the lost at all costs.

In modern society, sin has lost its sting. It has been diluted with psychological terms and referred to as weaknesses or illnesses. But the consequences of sin remain unchanged. Sin separates us from God, creates feelings of guilt and inferiority, and robs sinners of peace of mind.

Sin will eventually find you out.

Many try to ignore this reality. They believe they are the exception to the divine law that says, *"We reap what we sow."* People give little thought to the consequences of their sins. Sin can be exceedingly costly. We cannot fully calculate the amount of sadness and sorrow it has inflicted upon the world.

When you sin, you distance yourself from God by following your own path instead of His. Accepting Jesus Christ as your personal Redeemer and Savior and choosing to live in His presence is the only way to guard yourself against sin. You will experience true freedom through Him as the Holy Spirit empowers you to live victoriously and without guilt.

As those who are born again, we should be eager to share the truth that, throughout history, those who have welcomed Christ into their lives have found joy. Jesus Himself said, *"I am come that they might have life, and that they might have it more abundantly." (John 10:10)*. This means you can live in peace, knowing He is always with you.

Many people today are trapped by harmful habits and destructive choices. The living Christ offers them freedom, breaking the chains of sin. Others long for love, mercy, and compassion in a harsh and unforgiving world. Jesus still extends His grace to all who accept Him as their Redeemer and Savior.

When you welcome the Master into your life with the same excitement the people of Jerusalem felt, Christ's joy and peace will fill your heart.

You must look beyond your present circumstances to be an effective soul winner. Refuse to let limitations or distractions hinder you from this great calling. Remove anything that obstructs your focus and commit yourself wholeheartedly to serving the Lord in soul-winning this year—it is your purpose.

Soul winning is sharing the Word of God and giving others the opportunity to accept Christ, saving them from eternal separation from God. Through this, they enter into a relationship with Christ, experiencing His goodness and inheritance even in this life. As

Pastor Dr. Claudine Benjamin

Fanny Crosby beautifully wrote, soul winning is to *"Rescue the perishing and care for the dying."*

Though God uses individuals as His instruments in soul-winning, the work itself belongs to Him from beginning to end. Because it is His mission, we can have confidence that as we labor in evangelism, He will draw people to salvation. Above all, we must believe in the power of God to transform lives.

Chapter 1

Everyone Can Be a Soul Winner

To be an effective soul winner, certain requirements must be met—yet every child of God can fulfill them and lead others to Christ.

First and foremost, anyone seeking real success in bringing souls to Christ must know Him personally as their Savior. If we desire to lead others to Him, we must turn away from sin, worldliness, and selfishness, fully surrendering our hearts to Jesus. He must have complete lordship over our thoughts, purposes, actions, and entire lives. If we insist on our own way instead of yielding to Him, our ability to win souls will be hindered, and lives that could have been saved may be lost.

When Christ is truly honored in our lives, our ambitions fade, and God becomes the center of our minds and deeds. In this way, we become effective instruments in His hands.

To be a successful soul winner, I encourage you to develop these qualities: holiness of character, complete surrender to God, a deep and active spiritual life, daily consecration, humility, unwavering faith, and the anointing of the Holy Spirit.

Reasons for Being a Soul Winner

The most important reason for being a soul winner is that it is a commandment from God. Soul winning is not merely a church program or a strategy for growth—it is a direct mandate from the Lord Jesus to every believer. This makes soul-winning the greatest responsibility of every Christian.

When we say it is a *commandment*, what do we mean? A commandment is something that must be obeyed; it is not open for discussion, suggestion, or debate. In the same way that love is a commandment, so is soul-winning. It is time for us to rise to this calling and take the mission of evangelism seriously.

Jesus made this clear in **Matthew 28:18-19**: *"And Jesus came and spake unto them, saying, All power is given unto me in heaven and in earth. Go ye therefore, and teach all nations, baptizing them in the name of the Father, and of the Son, and of the Holy Ghost:"*

Another powerful reason to be a soul winner is the joy it brings in heaven. The Bible tells us that when one sinner repents, there is great rejoicing among the angels. Divine healing, deliverance, and other miracles are wonderful, but nothing brings greater joy in heaven than the salvation of a soul. Winning souls is not only pleasing to God—it is His greatest delight.

There is joy in heaven over every soul that repents. This is why you and I must be soul winners. When you lead someone to Christ, it brings joy to heaven. Thank God for divine healing, deliverance, and other good works, but what truly rejoices the heart of the Father is the salvation of souls. Winning souls is pleasurable to God, and it is right to say that the greatest joy in heaven comes from soul-winning.

Therefore, we must rise to this challenge and take evangelism seriously. Luke 10:7 says, *"And in the same house remain, eating and drinking such things as they give: for the labourer is worthy of his hire. Go not from house to house."* In Luke 10:10, Jesus instructs, *"But into whatsoever city ye enter, and they receive you not, go your ways out into the streets of the same, and say."*

Winning souls is our divine assignment. Let us embrace it wholeheartedly, knowing that each salvation brings joy to heaven. There are millions of people in the world who are still unsaved. This is why the mission of winning souls must be taken seriously.

Do you realize that many have never heard the gospel? Do you know that countless souls are heading toward a lost eternity? Even now, there are people who have yet to know Jesus Christ as their Lord and personal Savior.

This is why soul-winning is not optional—it is a divine mandate. Let this mission fill your heart and drive your actions, in the name of Jesus.

Every soul is eternal—it cannot die. When the body perishes and returns to dust, whether buried, cremated, or lost at sea, the soul continues to live. It will exist for all eternity.

Pastor Dr. Claudine Benjamin

Every soul has the potential to be transformed into the likeness of Christ. No matter how wretched a person may seem, they can be changed by the power and mercy of our loving God.

We are living testimonies of this truth. Once we were lost in sin, living reckless and meaningless lives. But the moment we chose to open our hearts to God, He reached down with His loving hands, rescued us from sin, cleansed and transformed us. Now, we walk the glory road!

Chapter 2

The Word, Prayer, and the Holy Spirit in Soul-Winning

If you are serious about winning souls, you must have a deep, working knowledge of the Word of God. The Bible calls it *"the sword of the Spirit"* (see Ephesians 6:17), which God uses to convict hearts, reveal Christ, and save men and women from eternal damnation.

We must rely on both the Word of God and the Holy Spirit to bring people to Christ. The Word reveals humanity's need for a Savior, presents Jesus as the only Savior, and shows the way to receive Him personally.

Knowing Christ as Savior equips believers to face the challenges of the Christian journey. To be truly effective in soul-winning, we must work in partnership with the Holy Spirit, who will guide us to the right Scriptures in each situation, leading souls to Christ.

We must always remember that the Holy Spirit convicts the sinner, converts the repentant, and consecrates the believer.

Salvation is entirely the work of the Holy Spirit. He uses us as instruments to minister to lost humanity, but His power transforms lives.

Prayer

If we desire success in bringing souls to Christ, prayer is essential—sincere, frequent, and intercessory prayer. Every step of soul-winning must be grounded in prayer.

First, we must ask God to lead us to the right people. He does not intend for us to speak to everyone we meet, as doing so could waste valuable time on those we are not meant to reach. Instead, we should seek His guidance, trusting Him to direct us to those whose hearts are ready.

Acts 8:29 says, *"Then the Spirit said unto Philip, Go near, and join thyself to this chariot."* This passage shows how the angel of the Lord directed Philip to the Ethiopian eunuch, leading to his salvation. In the same way, when we pray, God will guide us to those He has prepared to receive His Word.

Prayer Is Essential for Soul Winning

As we engage in soul-winning, we must seek the Lord's guidance. God's Spirit is always at work in people's lives, drawing them to Himself, and His power is available to us as we share the gospel.

We need to pray for His direction, asking Him to lead us to the right people at the right time. We must also rely on His power to overcome fear and to speak the right words with wisdom and boldness.

Because God knows every heart, He will guide us in what to say and which Bible passages to share with those He leads us to.

Experienced soul-winners can testify to moments when God directed them to specific verses of scripture they may not have chosen on their own, yet they were exactly what was needed at that time. When we rely on the Holy Spirit, He equips us with the right words to touch lives and bring souls to Christ.

The Power of Prayer in Soul-Winning

We must ask God for the right words to say and His power to make those words effective. It is not enough to have a message from God—we need His divine power to drive that message into the heart of the one we are witnessing to.

Soul-winners must learn this lesson through experience: we cannot convert a sinner by our own strength. But when we lift an earnest prayer for God's help, He hears us and provides the strength we need.

After we have done our part, we must trust God to continue the work. Regardless of whether our efforts seem successful or unsuccessful, we should commit each soul to God in prayer.

In today's busy world, one of the greatest needs for every worker is more time in prayer. Praying more does not mean working less; it means accomplishing far more through God's power.

Pastor Dr. Claudine Benjamin

The Holy Spirit

To be a successful soul-winner, you must be baptized with the Holy Spirit. Acts 1:8 declares: *"But ye shall receive power, after that the Holy Ghost is come upon you: and ye shall be witnesses unto me both in Jerusalem, and in all Judaea, and in Samaria, and unto the uttermost part of the earth."*

Jesus spoke these words to His disciples after giving them the Great Commission, instructing them to bring men and women to Him. The key to soul-winning power remains the same today—it comes after the Holy Spirit fills us.

On the Day of Pentecost, when the Holy Spirit came upon the disciples, over 3,000 souls were saved. This demonstrates that true evangelistic success is only possible through the power of the Holy Spirit.

You Shall Receive Power: The Holy Spirit and the Great Commission

Just before His ascension, Jesus appointed a meeting with His disciples on a mountainside in Galilee. This was possibly one of the most significant moments they would share with Him. It was here that He announced the church's mission statement—its marching orders.

On that day, Jesus outlined a plan for global evangelization, a mission so vital that it became known as the Great Commission. Who would have imagined that a quiet gathering on a Galilean mountainside would shape the course of history, establishing the benchmark for spreading the gospel worldwide?

The Urgency in Winning Souls

During this meeting, Jesus:

- Declared His authority.
- Issued His command.
- Outlined the plan of operation.
- Stated the disciples' obligation.
- Gave them their message.

He assured them of His eternal presence. His authority for the Commission was clear: *"All power is given unto me in heaven and in earth." (Matthew 28:18).*

As the omnipotent Son of God, He ensured that all the power of heaven and earth stood behind this divine mission. Jesus then gave the command: *"Go ye therefore, and teach all nations, baptizing them in the name of the Father, and of the Son, and of the Holy Ghost." (Matthew 28:19).*

He outlined the plan of operation: Go, teach all people everywhere, baptize them, and instruct them to observe all that He had commanded. He also emphasized their obligation—to follow and teach everything He had spoken. Finally, He gave them a promise that would stand for all time: *"Lo, I am with you always, even unto the end of the world. Amen." (Matthew 28:20).*

From Galilee, the disciples journeyed to the Mount of Ascension, and from there, they went to the upper room, remaining there until the Day of Pentecost had fully come. Each of the Gospel writers—Matthew, Mark, Luke, and John—recorded a version of the Great Commission

Matthew's Account

"Go ye therefore, and teach all nations, baptizing them in the name of the Father, and of the Son, and of the Holy Ghost: Teaching them to observe all things whatsoever I have commanded you: and, lo, I am with you always, even unto the end of the world. Amen." (Matthew 28:19-20).

Mark's Account

"Go ye into all the world, and preach the gospel to every creature. He that believeth and is baptized shall be saved; but he that believeth not shall be damned. And these signs shall follow them that believe; In my name shall they cast out devils; they shall speak with new tongues." (Mark 16:15-17).

The Power of the Holy Spirit in the Great Commission

Luke's Account

"And that repentance and remission of sins should be preached in his name among all nations, beginning at Jerusalem. And ye are witnesses of these things. And, behold, I send the promise of my Father upon you: but tarry ye in the city of Jerusalem, until ye be endued with power from on high." (Luke 24:47-49).

John's Account

"Then said Jesus to them again, Peace be unto you: as my Father hath sent me, even so send I you. And when he had said this, he breathed on them, and saith unto them, Receive ye the Holy Ghost." (John 20:21-22).

The Urgency in Winning Souls

Luke's Affirmation in the Book of Acts

"And, being assembled together with them, commanded them that they should not depart from Jerusalem, but wait for the promise of the Father, which, saith he, ye have heard of me. For John truly baptized with water; but ye shall be baptized with the Holy Ghost not many days hence. But ye shall receive power after that the Holy Ghost is come upon you: and ye shall be witnesses unto me both in Jerusalem, and in all Judaea, and in Samaria, and unto the uttermost part of the earth." (Acts 1:4-5, 8).

In the context of the Great Commission, we see the Holy Spirit's power and the necessity of the baptism in the Spirit for the fulfillment of this divine mission. The power of the Holy Ghost is the driving force behind the Great Commission.

Christ not only gave them the command to go, but He also commanded them to tarry: *"Go, but tarry."* They were not to leave Jerusalem until they were fully equipped. Jesus made it clear: *"You need to be endued with power from on high."* The Greek word for *endued* is *enduo*, which means *"to be clothed upon."* Jesus was essentially saying: *"Do not go until you are clothed with power from on high."*

The Holy Spirit's Role From Creation to Redemption

It is significant that the last message Jesus preached before His ascension was about the fullness of the Spirit—because the power to witness was not optional. It was a command: *"Do not go until you are filled."*

Pastor Dr. Claudine Benjamin

From Genesis to Revelation, the Holy Spirit has played a vital role in God's redemptive plan for humanity. The Bible opens with the words: *"In the beginning, God,"* and we see that the Spirit moved over the face of the deep. The plan of salvation was not an afterthought—Jesus was the Lamb slain from the foundation of the world.

Throughout scripture, we see the Holy Spirit at work, from creation to the end times. Even in the final book of the Bible, the Spirit continues His call to the lost: *"And the Spirit and the bride say, come . . . And whosoever will, let him take the water of life freely." (Revelation 22:17).*

The Work of the Holy Spirit in Reaching the Lost

The ministry of the Holy Spirit to the lost is clearly outlined by Jesus in John 16:7–11: *"Nevertheless I tell you the truth; It is expedient for you that I go away: for if I go not away, the Comforter will not come unto you; but if I depart, I will send him unto you. And when he is come, he will reprove the world of sin, and of righteousness, and of judgment: of sin, because they believe not on me; of righteousness, because I go to my Father, and ye see me no more; of judgment, because the prince of this world is judged."*

Jesus explains the essential role of the Holy Spirit in drawing sinners to salvation. The process of a sinner coming to Christ is set forth plainly here:

1. **Conviction of sin** – The Holy Spirit convicts sinners of their unbelief, revealing their need for Christ.

The Urgency in Winning Souls

2. **Revealing righteousness** – The Holy Spirit testifies of Christ's righteousness, showing that Jesus is the only way to the Father.

3. **Warning of judgment** – The Holy Spirit makes it clear that Satan has already been judged, and those who reject Christ will face judgment as well.

Without the Holy Spirit's work, no sinner would recognize their lost condition or their need for salvation. Through His divine conviction, hearts are softened and drawn toward Christ.

The Holy Spirit's Role in Salvation

The Holy Spirit plays a vital role in bringing sinners to Christ. He does this through three key functions:

1. **Conviction of sin** – The Holy Spirit reveals to sinners their lost condition, making them aware of their need for salvation. John 16:8 says, *"And when he is come, he will reprove the world of sin, and of righteousness, and of judgment."* No one can recognize their need for Christ until the Spirit reveals it.

2. **Drawing the sinner** – Jesus Himself declared, *"No man can come to me, except the Father which hath sent me draw him" (John 6:44a).* The Holy Spirit draws the sinner toward Christ, stirring their heart and awakening their spiritual need.

3. **Illumination through the Word** – The Holy Spirit uses the Word of God to open the eyes of sinners. Ephesians 1:18

speaks of this work: *"The eyes of your understanding being enlightened."* When the gospel is preached in the power of the Spirit, it penetrates hearts and brings people to repentance.

Biblical Examples of the Holy Spirit's Conviction

The New Testament provides clear instances where the Holy Spirit convicted sinners:

- Pentecost (see Acts 2:37) – Peter preached under the anointing of the Holy Spirit, and the people "were pricked in their heart" and cried out, "Men and brethren, what shall we do?" As a result, 3,000 souls were saved.

- Stephen's sermon (see Acts 7:54) – As Stephen proclaimed the truth, the people were "cut to the heart" in conviction. However, rather than surrender, they resisted the Spirit and stoned Stephen.

- Paul's conversion (Acts 9:3-5) – On the road to Damascus, Paul encountered Jesus in a divine revelation. Jesus told him, *"It is hard for thee to kick against the pricks,"* referring to the inner conviction Paul had been resisting.

The Power of the Holy Spirit in Evangelism

A preacher once asked how so many people were won to Christ through messages about the Holy Spirit. The answer is simple: it is not our power that saves, but the Holy Spirit working through us. When the Gospel is preached with the Spirit's power, it cuts through resistance and opens hearts to salvation.

The Holy Spirit's Work in Believer's Life for Soul-Winning

1. **Walking in the Spirit (see Romans 8:1-4)**

"There is therefore now no condemnation to them which are in Christ Jesus, who walk not after the flesh, but after the Spirit." (Romans 8:1).

Soul-winners must live Spirit-filled lives, free from the control of sin so they can be used by God effectively.

2. **Being Spiritually Minded (see Romans 8:5-8)**

A mind controlled by the Spirit seeks the things of God, which enables believers to have the heart and vision to win souls.

3. **Mortifying the Deeds of the Body (see Romans 8:13)**

Sin hinders evangelism. The Holy Spirit helps believers overcome fleshly desires, making them pure vessels for His use.

4. **Being Led by the Spirit (Romans 8:14)**

The Spirit guides believers to whom to witness to, just as He led Philip to the Ethiopian eunuch (see Acts 8:29).

5. **The Spirit of Adoption (Romans 8:15-16)**

As children of God, we have the assurance and confidence to share the Gospel, knowing that the Spirit is with us.

Pastor Dr. Claudine Benjamin

Ephesians: The Holy Spirit's Role in Strengthening Believers

In Ephesians, Paul highlights how the Spirit strengthens believers:

- **Sealing of the Holy Spirit (see Ephesians 1:13-14)** – The Spirit is the guarantee of our salvation, giving us boldness in witnessing.

- **Spiritual Wisdom and Revelation (see Ephesians 1:17-18)** – The Holy Spirit opens our understanding to God's will and gives us the wisdom to reach others.

- **Strengthening the Inner Man (see Ephesians 3:16-17)** – Evangelism requires spiritual strength, which comes from the Holy Spirit dwelling within us.

- **Being Filled with the Spirit (see Ephesians 5:18-19)** – A Spirit-filled believer overflows with joy and boldness to proclaim the Gospel.

The Holy Spirit is central to both the conviction of sinners and the empowerment of believers. Without His presence and power, soul-winning would be impossible. Jesus commanded His disciples to wait for the Spirit before beginning their mission (see Acts 1:8), and the same remains true today: to be effective soul-winners, we must be Spirit-filled and Spirit-led.

Paul emphasizes the essential role of the Holy Spirit in the life of a believer, culminating in the command found in *Ephesians 5:18: "And be not drunk with wine, wherein is excess; but be filled with the Spirit."*

The Urgency in Winning Souls

This verse serves as a call to continual reliance on the Holy Spirit, not just for personal sanctification but for effective ministry, including soul-winning. The entire book of Ephesians outlines the Spirit's work in believers:

1. **Sealed by the Spirit (see Ephesians 1:13-14).** The Holy Spirit is our guarantee of salvation, giving us confidence in our faith and witness.

2. **Made Alive by the Spirit (see Ephesians 2:1-5).** Just as we were dead in sin but made alive by the Spirit, we now carry the message of life to others.

3. **A Dwelling Place for God (see Ephesians 2:22).** As the Spirit lives in us, we become vessels for His presence, influencing those around us.

4. **Strengthened in the Inner Man (see Ephesians 3:16).** Spiritual endurance and boldness for evangelism come through the Spirit's power.

5. **Walking in the Fruit of the Spirit (see Ephesians 5:9).** Our lives should reflect the character of Christ, making our testimony effective.

6. **Filled with the Spirit (see Ephesians 5:18).** The key to a victorious Christian life and powerful witness is to be continually filled with the Spirit.

Pastor Dr. Claudine Benjamin

Paul's Conclusion: The Holy Spirit and Spiritual Warfare

In **Ephesians 6**, Paul ends with a strong reminder that believers are in a spiritual battle, and the Holy Spirit equips us for victory:

- **The Sword of the Spirit (see Ephesians 6:17)** – The Word of God is our offensive weapon in evangelism.

- **Praying in the Spirit (see Ephesians 6:18)** – Effective soul-winning requires Spirit-led prayer.

Paul's teaching on the Holy Spirit in Romans 8 and Ephesians makes it clear: the believer's life, power, and effectiveness in evangelism depend entirely on the Holy Spirit. If we desire to see lives transformed, we must walk in step with the Spirit, be filled with His power, and rely on Him completely. The works of the Holy Spirit in a believer's life are essential for being an effective witness and soul-winner. For Paul, this was not optional—believers could not fulfill the Great Commission without this fullness. In Ephesians 6:10, he exhorts them to *"be strong in the Lord, and in the power of His might."*

The Urgency and Work of the Holy Spirit in the Last Days

A great move of the Holy Spirit is unfolding in the world today, calling the church to fulfill the Great Commission in these last days. James, a leader in the early church, connected the final great harvest with the return of the Lord: *"Be patient therefore, brethren, unto the coming of the Lord. Behold, the husbandman waiteth for the precious fruit of the earth, and hath long patience for it, until he receive the early and latter rain." (James 5:7).*

We often speak of the "early rain" as the outpouring of the Holy Spirit on the Day of Pentecost and the "latter rain" as the last day's revival we are witnessing today. The early rain was for planting; the latter rain is for harvest. The Holy Spirit is preparing the church to reap an abundant harvest, equipping believers to fulfill Christ's mandate.

A little over a century ago, Spirit-filled believers were few, scattered in small pockets around the world. Today, demographers estimate that more than 600 million people testify to being Spirit-filled. An army of this size, empowered by the Spirit, has limitless potential. But time is short.

The Urgency of the Harvest

Some years ago, while visiting the U.S. Midwest, I held meetings during the wheat harvest season. When attendance was lower than expected, I asked a friend why so few people had come.

"This is harvest time," he explained.

After the service, he took me outside where I saw tractors moving across the vast plains, their lights glowing in the darkness.

"We run these tractors 24 hours a day," he told me. *"We eat in the fields. When one person is too exhausted to drive, another takes his place. We have to harvest the wheat now. In a few days, the cold winds will come, the ground will freeze, and the wheat will rust. If we wait too long, the harvest will be lost."*

Then he pointed to a house in the distance, *"Soon, the snow will be up to the eaves. Once that happens, it's over."*

These farmers understood urgency. They knew the cost of delay.

The Holy Spirit's Call to Action

The Holy Spirit, who knows the mind of Christ, moves His people with the same compassion that Jesus felt when He saw the multitudes—sheep without a shepherd. That compassion stirred Him to action.

Today, the Holy Spirit is awakening the church with that same urgency. The time for harvest is now. We must not wait. The night is coming, and soon, the opportunity will be gone.

Chapter 3

Love Them Into the Kingdom

Love is one of the most powerful and effective tools for winning souls into the kingdom of God. Without genuine love for people, our efforts will be mechanical and powerless.

We may know the right approach, words, and scriptures to share, but without love, our words will lack impact. A lost soul will not be moved by mere knowledge or technique; it is love that touches the heart and opens the door for transformation.

To truly reach the lost, we must carry the same love that Christ has for them—a love that sees beyond sin and brokenness and compels us to action. When we love as He loves, our words will carry the power of the Holy Spirit, and lives will be changed.

Like Paul, we should carry a "great heaviness and unceasing pain" in our hearts for the unsaved. When this burden grips us, our words and actions will reflect a deep earnestness that even the indifferent cannot ignore.

Pastor Dr. Claudine Benjamin

A true love for souls makes us constantly aware of opportunities to reach the lost. We will find them on the streets, in stores, homes, churches, schools—places we might have otherwise overlooked. Love sharpens our vision and compels us to act.

But how does one develop such a love for souls? Like every other grace in the Christian life, it is the work of the Holy Spirit. If we recognize that our love for the lost is lacking, we must humbly confess this to God. We must ask Him, through His Spirit, to fill our hearts with His love for people. When we ask, we must expect Him to answer—because it is His desire that none should perish.

1 John 5:14-15 encourages us to seek the help of the Holy Spirit: *"And this is the confidence that we have in him, that, if we ask anything according to his will, he heareth us: And if we know that he hears us, whatsoever we ask, we know that we have the petitions that we desired of him."*

Jesus Christ demonstrated an intense love for souls. In Matthew 23:37, we see His deep sorrow for Jerusalem: *"O Jerusalem, Jerusalem, thou that killest the prophets, and stonest them which are sent unto thee, how often would I have gathered thy children together, even as a hen gathereth her chickens under her wings, and ye would not!"*

This deep love for the lost was central to Christ's mission. It was the very reason He came to earth—to redeem lost humanity. And it is only through consistent companionship with Christ that we, too, receive this same burden for souls. As we walk closely with Him, He imparts His heart to us, filling us with the same love and urgency that defined His life and sacrifice. Feelings are the result of our thoughts. If we desire a particular feeling to grow in our lives—such as the passion to be a soul winner—we must dwell on the thoughts that nurture it.

Any believer who takes time to deeply consider the peril and misery of a soul separated from Christ will begin to grasp the immense worth of that soul in God's eyes. Reflecting on the love God demonstrated in offering His Son to redeem the lost will naturally stir an intense desire for their salvation.

Likewise, when we reflect on our own former condition—our lost and hopeless state without Christ—and on the great sacrifice He made to rescue us, our hearts will be filled with a longing to lead others to the Savior we have found. We are all called to live out the Great Commandment: to love God with all our heart, soul, mind, and strength and to love our neighbor as ourselves.

"We love Him because He first loved us." (1 John 4:19).

As we abide in Yeshua's love, His love flows through us, enabling us to love others—including our enemies. It is only through His love that we can truly fulfill this calling, reflecting His heart to the world around us.

Chapter 4

Soul Winning in the Family

When Jesus gave the command to go into all the world and preach the gospel, He didn't exclude our own homes. The urgency to win souls must begin with the people who know us best—our families. Before we can effectively reach strangers, we must first minister to the ones who sit around our dinner tables, share our DNA, and carry our family name.

There is no greater heartbreak than knowing your loved ones are lost. There is no greater joy than seeing them come to Christ. The family is the foundation of society, and when our families are won to Christ, we strengthen the body of Christ and secure a generational legacy.

The Family: Our First Mission Field

Jesus told the man delivered from demons in Luke 8:39a, *"Return to thine own house, and shew how great things God hath done unto thee."* That is where the testimony begins—at home.

When you are truly transformed by the gospel, your family will notice. They may not always respond the way you hope, but your life becomes the sermon they can't stop hearing.

Biblical Examples of Family Salvation

1. **Noah (see Genesis 7:1)**

God told Noah, *"Come thou and all thy house into the ark; for thee have I seen righteous before me in this generation."* Noah's obedience to God led to the salvation of his entire household.

2. **Lot (see Genesis 19:12-14)**

Lot was warned of judgment and urged to get his family out. Though some hesitated or rejected the warning, he was responsible for reaching them. He interceded, pleaded, and obeyed God's direction to save as many as possible.

3. **Cornelius (see Acts 10:24, 44)**

Cornelius gathered his whole household to hear Peter's message. As the Word was preached, the Holy Spirit fell on everyone in the house—demonstrating that family revival is possible!

4. **The Philippian Jailer (see Acts 16:31-34)**

Paul and Silas declared, *"Believe on the Lord Jesus Christ, and thou shalt be saved, and thy house."* That very night, the jailer and all his family were baptized. One man's encounter with Christ changed his entire home.

Why Family Soul-Winning Is Crucial

- **Responsibility:** As believers, we are accountable for sharing the gospel with our loved ones.

- **Influence:** Our families witness our character, lifestyle, and response to trials. That influence is powerful.

- **Opportunity:** We often have more access to our family than anyone else does. Use that access wisely and prayerfully.

- **Legacy:** When you win one family member, you often open the door for others to come to Christ too.

When It's Difficult

It can be painful when your own family rejects your faith. Jesus said in Matthew 13:57, *"A prophet is not without honour, save in his own country, and in his own house."* Don't be discouraged. Keep sowing. Keep praying. Your witness is not in vain.

Sometimes it is not your words that will win them—it is your walk. Let your actions speak. Stay consistent. Let them see your peace, joy, love, and perseverance. The gospel lived out is often more powerful than the gospel preached.

What You Can Do

1. **Pray daily and strategically.** Don't just pray *"Lord, save them"*—pray specifically. Ask God to remove spiritual blinders, to send laborers, and to soften their hearts.

2. **Live with integrity.** Be the same person at home that you are at church. Hypocrisy turns people away; authenticity draws them in.

3. **Share when led.** Don't force it. Be sensitive to the Holy Spirit. Sometimes a well-timed testimony or scripture can open a door.

4. **Fast for breakthrough.** Fasting adds power to your prayers. It aligns you with God's will and brings clarity and breakthrough.

5. **Refuse to give up.** Don't stop praying. Don't stop loving. Don't stop believing.

Reflection

- Who in your family still needs to be saved?
- What barriers exist that hinder them from coming to Christ?
- What can you do this week to share God's love with them?

Acts 16:31 declares, *"Believe on the Lord Jesus Christ, and thou shalt be saved, and thy house."* This promise is both a comfort and a calling. It compels us to stand in the gap for our families, to pray fervently, witness boldly, and live righteously before them.

Too often, we overlook the spiritual needs of those closest to us because of familiarity or strained relationships. But love demands persistence. The love of Christ should compel us to keep interceding, sharing, and living as a light in the midst of darkness.

Why Family First?

- **Covenant responsibility:** We are stewards over our homes (see Joshua 24:15).

- **Influence and access:** We have daily opportunities to demonstrate the gospel in word and deed.

- **Legacy and generational impact:** Soul winning within the family sets a foundation for future generations.

Practical Steps

1. **Live the Gospel:** Let your life preach louder than your words.

2. **Pray strategically:** Call out each family member's name in prayer. Ask God for specific strategies to reach them.

3. **Speak the truth in love:** Avoid arguments; plant seeds and trust the Holy Spirit to water them.

4. **Create a spiritual atmosphere:** Fill your home with praise, the Word, and testimonies.

5. **Fast for breakthrough:** Some spiritual strongholds are only broken through fasting and prayer (see Matthew 17:21).

Don't give up if they reject you; remember, they rejected Christ first. Stay faithful. Even if you don't see change right away, know

Pastor Dr. Claudine Benjamin

that your labor is not in vain. The seeds you are planting will bear fruit in due season.

Chapter 5

Soul Winning in the Workplace

The workplace is one of the most overlooked mission fields in the modern church. Christians often separate their spiritual life from their professional life, not realizing that God may have strategically placed them in their jobs for a higher purpose: to be a witness.

Your job is not just a means of income—it is a divine assignment. Souls are lost in the streets, boardrooms, break rooms, and office halls. Every believer should view their workplace as an opportunity to plant seeds of salvation.

The Mission Field You Clock Into

Jesus said in Matthew 5:14–16, *"Ye are the light of the world. A city that is set on an hill cannot be hid ... Let your light so shine before men, that they may see your good works, and glorify your Father which is in heaven."*

You may not be allowed to preach a sermon at work, but your life is a sermon. Your attitude, work ethic, compassion, and integrity all speak volumes. In many workplaces, you might be the only Bible some people will ever read.

Overcoming Fear and Boundaries

Yes, there are restrictions in professional environments, and wisdom must be exercised. However, being wise doesn't mean being silent. You don't need a pulpit—you need sensitivity to the Holy Spirit.

Here are a few ways to witness wisely at work:

1. **Build genuine relationships** – Evangelism begins with connection. Let people know you care.

2. **Be consistent** – Show integrity, humility, and excellence in your work. That earns trust and respect.

3. **Pray for your coworkers** – Intercession is a secret weapon. Ask God to open doors and prepare hearts.

4. **Look for natural openings** – People often open up about personal struggles. Offer encouragement, and be ready to share your faith.

5. **Offer to pray** – When someone is sick, stressed, or hurting, offer a simple *"Can I pray with you?"* It's often welcomed, and it opens the door for the Gospel.

A Witness in Word and Deed

Colossians 3:23 reminds us, *"And whatsoever ye do, do it heartily, as to the Lord, and not unto men."*

When you work as unto the Lord, you reflect Christ. When you honor leadership, keep your word, avoid gossip, and stay joyful under pressure—people notice. These moments become open doors for witness.

Paul was a tentmaker, Lydia was a businesswoman, and Daniel worked in government. God used all in their vocational roles. Your workplace matters to the kingdom.

Planting, Watering and Harvesting

You may not lead your co-worker to Christ on the first conversation, but you may be the one who plants the seed. Another may water it. And, in God's timing, someone will reap the harvest (see 1 Corinthians 3:6–7).

Be faithful. Be prayerful. Be bold. Souls are hanging in the balance—even in your workplace.

Reflection Section

Personal Reflection Questions

1. Do you view your job as a spiritual assignment or just a paycheck?

2. How do your character and work ethic reflect Christ to your coworkers?

3. Who in your workplace may be going through something and needs hope?

4. Have you asked God for opportunities to witness at work?

5. What fears do you need to surrender in order to be a bold witness?

Action Step

Identify one person in your workplace and begin to pray for their salvation daily. Look for an opportunity to plant a seed—through kindness, conversation, or testimony.

Scripture Reference List: Soul Winning in the Workplace

- Matthew 5:14–16 – Letting your light shine before others.
- Colossians 3:23 – Working as unto the Lord.
- 1 Corinthians 3:6–7 – Planting, watering, and harvesting.
- Romans 1:16 – Not ashamed of the Gospel.
- Ecclesiastes 9:10 – Doing your work with all your might.
- Daniel 6:3–5 – Daniel's excellent spirit in the workplace.
- Acts 16:14 – Lydia, a businesswoman used by God.
- Proverbs 11:30 – He who wins souls is wise.

Chapter 6

How Do I Begin as a Soul Winner?

The first question many ask is, "How do I start?" The answer is simple—just begin. Regardless of who the person is, engaging them in a conversation about faith is easier than it seems.

A good starting point is to ask if they are a Christian or use a direct but gentle question, such as, "Are you saved?" or "Do you have a personal relationship with God?" Even when speaking with a total stranger, it is not difficult to steer the conversation toward spiritual matters. A casual discussion about current events or shared experiences can naturally lead to deeper topics. Jesus demonstrated this beautifully in His conversation with the Samaritan woman in John 4, beginning with a simple request for water before revealing profound spiritual truths.

Sometimes, the best approach is to bring up the subject immediately. A straightforward yet courteous question—"Are you a Christian?" or "Have you ever thought about where you stand with God?"—can spark reflection, even in those who seem indifferent. People often respond more openly than expected when approached with sincerity and humility. In fact, it is remarkable how frequently those who depend on God's leading find hearts already prepared for the message—and how rarely they face rejection.

However, in many cases, it is wise to build a connection first. Winning someone's trust and friendship can create an open door for sharing the gospel. Choose someone to pray for, cultivate a relationship with kindness, and ask the most important question of all when the right moment comes—"Would you like to know Christ personally?"

A wisely chosen tract placed in someone's hand can often serve as a natural opening for a spiritual conversation. Many times, you will encounter people whose faces reveal unhappiness or discontent. In such moments, a simple question—"Are you happy?"—can open the door to deeper discussion. If they answer no, you can gently respond, "I know Someone who can bring true happiness if you are willing to receive Him."

The ability to start these conversations will develop with practice. At first, you may feel awkward or unsure, but with time and experience, it will become easier and more natural.

Determining Where They Stand

Once the conversation begins, the first step is to understand where the person stands spiritually. This will help you respond wisely and appropriately to their needs. The following chapters will explore different types of individuals you may encounter, but here are some key questions that can guide your conversation:

- Are you saved?
- Are you a Christian?

The Urgency in Winning Souls

- Do you know that your sins can be forgiven?
- Do you know that you can have eternal life?
- Are you openly confessing Christ before the world?
- Have you been born again?

While some may answer these questions untruthfully—either out of ignorance or a desire to mislead—you can still gain valuable insight from their responses. The way they answer often reveals much about their understanding and spiritual condition.

Above all, be open to the leading of the Holy Spirit. If we rely on Him, He will often reveal a person's spiritual condition and guide us to the scriptures they need to hear.

Once we understand where someone stands, the next step is to lead them to accept Jesus Christ as their personal Savior and Lord. It is important to remember that our primary goal is not to persuade them to join a church, change their habits, or adopt a new lifestyle. Rather, our mission is to help them encounter Jesus Christ—the One who bore their sins in His own body on the cross. Through Him, they can receive immediate forgiveness and salvation.

Accepting Christ means more than simply believing in Him; it is a surrender of the heart. He must become their Master, guiding their thoughts, feelings, purposes, and actions. True transformation begins with this surrender, and the Holy Spirit will complete the work in their lives.

After leading someone to accept Christ, the next crucial step is to show them—through God's Word—that they have received forgiveness of sins and eternal life. Scripture provides clear assurance of this truth:

Acts 10:43 – "To him give all the prophets witness, that through his name whosoever believeth in him shall receive remission of sins."
John 3:36 – "He that believeth on the Son hath everlasting life: and he that believeth not the Son shall not see life; but the wrath of God abideth on him."

Grounding new believers in these biblical promises is vital so they can stand firm in their faith.

Additionally, they need guidance on how to grow and succeed in their new Christian life. Encouraging them to read and apply God's Word, pray daily, and seek fellowship with other believers will help them remain strong in their walk with Christ.

Above all, every step of leading someone to Christ should be rooted in scripture. The Word of God is the foundation of true salvation and discipleship.

Chapter 7

†

Open-Hearted

Many people are ready to give their lives to the Lord but simply do not know how. Helping them find the way to Christ is not difficult when we guide them with Scripture.

Isaiah 53:6 clearly reveals the path to salvation, *"All we like sheep have gone astray; we have turned, every one, to his own way;"*

Ask the person: "Is this true of you? Have you, like a lost sheep, gone your own way?" If they recognize this in their own life, you have the opportunity to show them God's solution.

Next, direct their attention to what God has done with their sins. Read the rest of the verse: *"and the Lord hath laid on him the iniquity of us all."*

Then ask: "What does this mean for you? What must you do to be saved?"

After reading the verse, you can ask the person you are witnessing to: "Does God give the power to become a child of God?" "What must you do to become a child of God?" "Receive Him." "Will you receive Him as your Savior and Master now?"

Isaiah 55:7 and John 3:16 are also powerful verses that clearly explain the way of salvation.

Isaiah 55:7 states, *"Let the wicked forsake his way, and the unrighteous man his thoughts: and let him return unto the Lord, and He will have mercy upon him; and to our God, for He will abundantly pardon."*

John 3:16 clearly expresses God's love and the promise of salvation, *"For God so loved the world, that He gave His only begotten Son, that whosoever believeth in Him should not perish, but have everlasting life."*

A powerful comparison can be made with Numbers 21:8-9, which illustrates the simplicity of faith and salvation, *"And the Lord said unto Moses, Make thee a fiery serpent, and set it upon a pole: and it shall come to pass, that every one that is bitten, when he looketh upon it, shall live. And Moses made a serpent of brass, and put it upon a pole, and it came to pass, that if a serpent had bitten any man, when he beheld the serpent of brass, he lived."*

Just as the Israelites were healed by looking at the bronze serpent in faith, so too must we look to Christ for salvation.

Another excellent verse to use in witnessing is Romans 1:16, *"For I am not ashamed of the gospel of Christ: for it is the power of God unto salvation to everyone that believeth; to the Jew first, and also to the Greek."*

The Urgency in Winning Souls

This verse emphasizes the power of the gospel and its availability to all who believe. You might ask the inquirer, *"According to this verse, who is the writer referring to?"* The answer is, *"Everyone who believes."* Then follow up with, *"What, then, is necessary for one to be saved?"* The response is simple: *"to believe."* Next, ask, *"Believe what?"* The answer is *"the gospel."*

1 Corinthians 15:3-4 provides the answer: *"For I delivered unto you first of all that which I also received, how that Christ died for our sins according to the scriptures; And that he was buried, and that he rose again the third day according to the scriptures."*

These verses clearly show that Christ died for our sins, was buried, and rose again on the third day. This is what a person must believe to be saved. Salvation comes from believing in the heart that Christ died for their sins and that He rose again from the dead.

When witnessing, ask: *"Do you believe that Christ died for your sins?"* and *"Do you believe that He rose again?"* If the person responds, *"Yes,"* follow up with, *"Will you, by faith, ask God to forgive your sins for Christ's sake?"*

Romans 10:13 assures us of this promise, *"For whosoever shall call upon the name of the Lord shall be saved."* This verse makes it clear—salvation is available to anyone who calls upon the Lord. Now, you can ask the most important question, *"Are you ready to call upon the Lord for salvation and trust that He saves you as He promises?"*

The way of salvation is also made plain through Exodus 12:7, 13, and 23, which foreshadows Christ's sacrifice.

Pastor Dr. Claudine Benjamin

Exodus 12:7, "And they shall take of the blood, and strike it on the two side posts and on the upper door post of the houses, wherein they shall eat it."

Exodus 12:13, "And the blood shall be to you for a token upon the houses where ye are: and when I see the blood, I will pass over you, and the plague shall not be upon you to destroy you, when I smite the land of Egypt."

Exodus 12:23, *"For the Lord will pass through to smite the Egyptians; and when he seeth the blood upon the lintel, and on the two side posts, the Lord will pass over the door, and will not suffer the destroyer to come in unto your houses to smite you."*

Just as the Israelites were spared from judgment by the blood of the lamb on their doorposts, we are saved from God's judgment by the blood of Christ. His sacrifice is the ultimate fulfillment of this Passover promise—when God sees the blood of Jesus applied to our lives, through faith, He grants us salvation and passes over our sins. These verses show that it was the blood that made the Israelites safe. The same is true today—the shed blood of Jesus makes us safe. When God sees the blood, He passes over us, sparing us from judgment. The only thing we must do is get under the blood.

To help the inquirer understand this, explain that the way to be under the blood is through faith in Jesus Christ and His shed blood on Calvary.

A Powerful Illustration: The Pharisee and the Publican

Another important Scripture reveals what a person may have and still be lost (like the Pharisee) and what a person may lack and still be saved (like the Publican).

Luke 18:10-13, *"Two men went up into the temple to pray; the one a Pharisee, and the other a publican. The Pharisee stood and prayed thus with himself, 'God, I thank thee, that I am not as other men are, extortioners, unjust, adulterers, or even as this publican. I fast twice in the week, I give tithes of all that I possess.' And the publican, standing afar off, would not lift up so much as his eyes unto heaven, but smote upon his breast, saying, 'God be merciful to me a sinner.'*

This passage makes a crucial point: Salvation is not about what we do but about recognizing our need for God's mercy. The Pharisee trusted in his own righteousness, but the Publican humbly acknowledged his sin and cried out for mercy.

Luke 18:14 concludes the parable with a powerful truth, *"I tell you, this man went down to his house justified rather than the other: for every one that exalteth himself shall be abased; and he that humbleth himself shall be exalted."*

Just as the Publican did, a person must acknowledge their sinfulness and cry out to God for mercy. When they do, they will go down to their house justified—forgiven and made right with God.

If you are witnessing to someone, ask: *"Will you do as the Publican did? Will you acknowledge your need for mercy and call upon God here and now?"*

When they do, follow up with: *"Do you believe God's Word that you are now justified?"*

Another Illustration of Saving Faith

Saving faith is beautifully illustrated in Luke 7:45-50, *"Thou gavest me no kiss: but this woman since the time I came in hath not ceased to kiss my feet. My head with oil thou didst not anoint: but this woman hath anointed my feet with ointment. Wherefore I say unto thee, Her sins, which are many, are forgiven; for she loved much: but to whom little is forgiven, the same loveth little. And he said unto her, Thy sins are forgiven. And they that sat at meat with him began to say within themselves, Who is this that forgiveth sins also? And he said to the woman, 'Thy faith hath saved thee; go in peace.'"*

Luke 7:50 tells us that this woman had "saving faith." She believed that Jesus could and would forgive her sins if she came to Him in faith. This is what saving faith is—trusting in Christ alone for salvation.

Galatians 3:10-13 also makes the way of salvation clear. Verse 10 describes the sinner's position before accepting Christ—under the curse of the law. Verse 13 reveals what Christ has done—He took that curse upon Himself. The only thing a sinner must do is accept Christ.

Galatians 3:10-13, *"For as many as are of the works of the law are under the curse: for it is written, Cursed is everyone that continueth not in all things which are written in the book of the law to do them. But that no man is justified by the law in the sight of God, it is evident: for, The just shall live by faith. And the law is not of faith: but, The man that doeth them shall live in them. Christ hath redeemed us from the curse of the law, being made a curse for us: for it is written, Cursed is every one that hangeth on a tree."*

Through Christ's sacrifice, we are redeemed. We are no longer under the law's curse but are justified by faith alone.

Chapter 8

†

Ones With Difficulties

"I am a Great Sinner"

Many people desire to be saved and understand how, yet they face obstacles that keep them from making that decision. One of the most common difficulties I have encountered while witnessing is the belief that they are too great a sinner—that they have gone too far in sin and cannot return.

1 Timothy 1:15 answers this objection fully, *"This is a faithful saying, and worthy of all acceptation, that Christ Jesus came into the world to save sinners; of whom I am chief."*

Luke 19:10 is another powerful passage to share in this situation. You can say, *"I have a passage intended especially for you. If you truly mean what you say, then you are exactly the person Jesus is seeking."*

"For the Son of man is come to seek and to save that which was lost." (Luke 19:10).

Romans 5:6-8 and Matthew 9:12-13 are also effective verses to emphasize God's love and purpose for sinners.

Pastor Dr. Claudine Benjamin

Romans 5:6-8, "For when we were yet without strength, in due time Christ died for the ungodly. For scarcely for a righteous man will one die: yet peradventure for a good man some would even dare to die. But God commendeth his love toward us, in that, while we were yet sinners, Christ died for us."

Matthew 9:12-13, "But when Jesus heard that, he said unto them, They that be whole need not a physician, but they that are sick. But go ye and learn what that meaneth, I will have mercy, and not sacrifice: for I am not come to call the righteous, but sinners to repentance."

These verses make it clear: no one is too great a sinner for Christ to save. In fact, He came specifically for those who recognize their need for Him.

Romans 10:13 and John 3:16 both emphasize the word "whosoever," highlighting that the offer of salvation is open to everyone, regardless of their background or past actions.

For those who have committed terrible sins and believe they can never be forgiven, Isaiah 1:18, 1 John 4:14, and Psalm 51:14 are especially powerful passages to share.

Isaiah 1:18, "Come now, and let us reason together, saith the Lord: though your sins be as scarlet, they shall be as white as snow; though they be red like crimson, they shall be as wool."

1 John 4:14, "And we have seen and do testify that the Father sent the Son to be the Saviour of the world."

Psalm 51:14, "Deliver me from bloodguiltiness, O God, thou God of my salvation: and my tongue shall sing aloud of thy righteousness."

These verses provide undeniable assurance that no sin is too great for God's mercy. He invites all to come to Him, no matter how broken or unworthy they may feel.

Never tell anyone that their sins are not great. Instead, acknowledge that their sins are greater than they may even realize. However, the good news is that every one of them has already been settled through the sacrificial death, burial, and resurrection of Jesus Christ.

Two powerful scriptures that reinforce this truth are:

- *Isaiah 53:6, "All we like sheep have gone astray; we have turned every one to his own way; and the Lord hath laid on him the iniquity of us all."*

- *1 Peter 2:24, "Who his own self bare our sins in his own body on the tree, that we, being dead to sins, should live unto righteousness: by whose stripes ye were healed."*

These verses remind us that while our sins are great, Christ's sacrifice is greater. He has already carried the burden of our iniquity, offering complete forgiveness and new life to all who trust in Him.

Failure

Another common difficulty people face is the fear of failure. Many say, *"I am afraid I won't be able to hold on."* However, 1 Peter 1:5 reassures us that we do not keep ourselves in the faith—it is God who keeps us: *"Who are kept by the power of God through faith unto salvation ready to be revealed in the last time."*

Similarly, John 10:28-29 shows that the security of a believer does not depend on their own strength but on the keeping power of the Father and the Son: *"And I give unto them eternal life; and they shall never perish, neither shall any man pluck them out of my hand. My Father, which gave them me, is greater than all; and no man is able to pluck them out of my Father's hand."*

2 Timothy 1:12 further emphasizes that it is Christ's responsibility—not ours—to keep what has been entrusted to Him: *"For the which cause I also suffer these things: nevertheless I am not ashamed: for I know whom I have believed, and am persuaded that he is able to keep that which I have committed unto him against that day."*

Other encouraging scriptures, such as Isaiah 41:10-13, 2 Chronicles 32:7-8, and Romans 14:4,11, remind us to be strong, courageous, and unafraid because God is with us, fighting our battles. When people in the Bible heard these words, they rested in the promise of God's protection.

For those afraid that temptation may cause them to fail, 1 Corinthians 10:13 is a powerful reminder of God's faithfulness: *"There hath no temptation taken you but such as is common to man: but God is faithful, who will not suffer you to be tempted above that ye are able; but will with the temptation also make a way to escape, that ye may be able to bear it."*

The message is clear: Our security is not in ourselves but in God's power. He is faithful to keep us, strengthen us, and provide a way through every trial. Like the people of Judah who "rested" in God's promise, we too can rest in the assurance that He will never fail us.

God's Presence and Strength in Times of Fear

The Bible consistently encourages us to be strong, courageous, and unafraid because God is with us, fighting our battles. Isaiah 4:1-6 portrays God's protection and provision for His people, promising a refuge and covering for those who trust in Him. Isaiah 13:2 calls believers to stand boldly, lifting a banner as a testimony to God's power. 2 Chronicles 32:7-8a records the words of Hezekiah to the people of Judah when they faced a powerful enemy: *"Be strong and courageous, be not afraid nor dismayed for the king of Assyria, nor for all the multitude that is with him: for there be more with us than with him: With him is an arm of flesh; but with us is the Lord our God to help us, and to fight our battles."*

The response of the people is just as important: *"And the people rested themselves upon the words of Hezekiah king of Judah." (2 Chronicles 32:8b).*

This passage is a powerful reminder that our confidence is not in human strength but in God's power. Romans 14:4 reassures believers that God is the one who upholds us: *"Who art thou that judgest another man's servant? to his own master he standeth or falleth. Yea, he shall be holden up: for God is able to make him stand."* Romans 14:11 reminds us of the ultimate authority of God, before whom all will one day bow: *"For it is written, As I live, saith the Lord, every knee shall bow to me, and every tongue shall confess to God."*

God's Faithfulness in Temptation

For those afraid that temptation may cause them to fail, 1 Corinthians 10:13 is a powerful reassurance of God's faithfulness: *"There hath no temptation taken you but such as is common to man: but God is faithful, who will not suffer you to be tempted above that ye are able; but will with the temptation also make a way to escape, that ye may be able to bear it."*

I Am Too Weak

Another difficulty some people face is the belief that they are too weak to overcome temptation or stand firm in their faith. The enemy constantly whispers that they lack the strength to endure. However, the Word of God has the answer.

2 Corinthians 12:9-10 teaches that God's strength is made perfect in our weakness. Apostle Paul faced a great trial and asked God three times to remove it. But God responded: *"My grace is sufficient for thee: for my strength is made perfect in weakness. Most gladly therefore will I rather glory in my infirmities, that the power of Christ may rest upon me. Therefore I take pleasure in infirmities, in reproaches, in necessities, in persecutions, in distresses for Christ's sake: for when I am weak, then am I strong."*

Where is Christ's strength made perfect? In weakness. The weaker we are in ourselves, the better because it allows us to fully rely on His strength. Similarly, Philippians 4:13 assures us: *"I can do all things through Christ which strengtheneth me."* No matter how weak we feel, we are never alone—Christ Himself gives us the strength we need. Additionally, 1 Corinthians 10:13 reminds us that God knows our weaknesses and will never allow us to be tempted beyond what we can bear: *"There hath no temptation taken you but such as is common to man: but God is faithful, who will not suffer you to be tempted above that ye are able; but will with the temptation also make a way to escape, that ye may be able to bear it."*

Strength in Christ Alone

Our weakness is not a disadvantage—it is an opportunity for God's power to be displayed in our lives. When we rely on Him, we find true strength, and He will always provide the grace we need to endure.

No matter the hardship or circumstances, those who dedicate their lives to Christ will find strength and endurance through Him. Philippians 4:13 reassures us that we are fully capable of overcoming sin through Christ's power. He calls us to live righteously and equips us with the strength to do so.

When we rely on Jesus, He empowers us to persevere through difficult times and break free from sinful habits we once thought impossible to overcome.

What Will Others Say?

One of the greatest concerns people have about following Christ is: *"What will others say about me if I become a Christian?"* or *"I will be persecuted if I follow Jesus."* It is important never to mislead anyone by saying they won't face challenges. Instead, we should show them that Scripture makes it clear—persecution is part of the Christian walk but also leads to eternal glory.

2 Timothy 2:12 reminds us: *"If we suffer, we shall also reign with him: if we deny him, he also will deny us."* Similarly, 2 Timothy 3:12 states: *"Yea, and all that will live godly in Christ Jesus shall suffer persecution."* Jesus Himself encouraged those who are persecuted for their faith in Matthew 5:10-12: *"Blessed are they which are persecuted for righteousness' sake: for theirs is the kingdom of heaven. Blessed are ye, when men shall revile you, and persecute you, and shall say all manner of evil against you falsely, for my sake. Rejoice and be exceeding glad: for great is your reward in heaven: for so persecuted they the prophets which were before you."*

Even though suffering may come, Romans 8:18 reassures us: *"...the sufferings of this present time are not worthy to be compared with the glory that shall be revealed in us."*

Persecution for Christ is not just a burden—it is a privilege. Hebrews 12:3 encourages us to look to Jesus, who endured far more than we ever will, as our source of strength and victory.

The Cost and Reward of Following Christ

Living out your faith in certain environments may be difficult—perhaps even in your current job or social circles. But consider the words of Jesus in Mark 8:36: *"For what shall it profit a man, if he shall gain the whole world, and lose his own soul?"* This verse highlights the immeasurable value of a person's soul. No earthly success, wealth, or approval can compare to the eternal life found in Christ.

Jesus provides further assurance in Matthew 6:33: *"But seek ye first the kingdom of God, and his righteousness; and all these things shall be added unto you."* Here, Jesus promises that if we put God and His kingdom first, He will meet our needs. He is a faithful provider, ensuring we lack nothing essential as we follow Him.

Commitment to Following Christ

In Matthew 16:24-27, Jesus teaches the necessity of self-denial and commitment in following Him: *"Then said Jesus unto his disciples, If any man will come after me, let him deny himself, and take up his cross, and follow me. For whosoever will save his life shall lose it: and whosoever will lose his life for my sake shall find it. For what is a man profited, if he shall gain the whole world, and lose his own soul? or what shall a man give in exchange for his soul? For the Son of man shall come in the glory of his Father with his angels; and then he shall reward every man according to his works."*

Here, Jesus underscores that following Him requires full commitment. True discipleship demands self-denial and a willingness to endure hardship for His sake. In the end, the reward of eternal life far outweighs the temporary gains of this world.

The Danger of Materialism

Similarly, Luke 12:16-21 warns against the dangers of placing wealth above God: *"And he spake a parable unto them, saying, The ground of a certain rich man brought forth plentifully: And he thought within himself, saying, What shall I do, because I have no room where to bestow my fruits? And he said, This will I do: I will pull down my barns, and build greater; and there will I bestow all my fruits and my goods. And I will say to my soul, Soul, thou hast much goods laid up for many years; take thine ease, eat, drink, and be merry. But God said unto him, Thou fool, this night thy soul shall be required of thee: then whose shall those things be, which thou hast provided? So is he that layeth up treasure for himself, and is not rich toward God."*

This passage reminds us that an obsession with material wealth can blind us to our spiritual needs. If we place our security in earthly riches rather than in God, we risk losing everything when we stand before Him. Our lives are not our own, and we do not know when we will be called to give an account.

A Call to True Riches

Ultimately, our focus should not be on accumulating wealth but on building a relationship with God. True riches come from being "rich toward God"—living a life of faith, obedience, and devotion. Let us remember that the treasures of this world are temporary, but the rewards of following Christ are eternal.

Too Much to Give Up?

Some may feel that following Christ requires sacrificing too much. However, the Bible makes it clear that what we gain in Christ far outweighs anything we leave behind. In Mark 8:36, Jesus poses a sobering question: *"For what shall it profit a man, if he shall gain the whole world, and lose his own soul?"*

No amount of wealth, status, or earthly success is worth the loss of eternal life. True fulfillment is found in surrendering to Christ, not in clinging to temporary gains. Paul echoes this truth in Philippians 3:7-8: *"But what things were gain to me, those I counted loss for*

Christ. Yea doubtless, and I count all things but loss for the excellency of the knowledge of Christ Jesus my Lord: for whom I have suffered the loss of all things, and do count them but dung, that I may win Christ."

Once a man of great status, Paul recognized that everything he once valued was worthless compared to knowing Christ. His words challenge us to reconsider what we hold dear and to embrace the surpassing worth of a life devoted to Jesus.

Moreover, Psalm 16:11 reassures us of the ultimate reward: *"Thou wilt shew me the path of life: in thy presence is fullness of joy; at thy right hand there are pleasures for evermore."*

Following Christ is not about loss but about gain—eternal joy, fulfillment, and the presence of God Himself. The sacrifices we make are nothing in comparison to the riches of His kingdom.

God Only Asks Us to Give Up What Harms Us

God never asks us to give up anything that is truly good for us. Instead, He calls us to let go of what is harmful—things that keep us from experiencing His best.

Psalm 84:11 reassures us of God's goodness: *"For the Lord God is a sun and shield: the Lord will give grace and glory: no good thing will he withhold from them that walk uprightly."* God is our protector and provider. He does not withhold blessings from those who follow Him; rather, He leads us toward what is truly good.

Likewise, Romans 8:32 reminds us of the depth of God's generosity: *"He that spared not his own Son, but delivered him up for us all, how shall he not with him also freely give us all things?"* If God was willing to sacrifice His own Son for our salvation, we can trust that He will also provide everything we need. Following Him does not mean losing out—it means gaining something far greater.

God's commands are not meant to deprive us but to protect us and lead us into the abundant life He has planned. When we surrender to Him, we discover that what He gives is always better than what we leave behind.

Do you want to hold on to anything that is ultimately not good for you? It is far better to willingly let go of worldly things and come to Christ without delay. People tend to cling to the things of this world, even though Scripture declares them worthless. They are temporary, fleeting, and, in the end, harmful to the soul.

1 John 2:17, "And the world passeth away, and the lust thereof: but he that doeth the will of God abideth for ever."

Jesus illustrates this truth in the parable of the rich fool: Luke 12:16-21, *"And he spake a parable unto them, saying, The ground of a certain rich man brought forth plentifully: And he thought within himself, saying, What shall I do, because I have no room where to bestow my fruits? And he said, This will I do: I will pull down my barns, and build greater; and there will I bestow all my fruits and my goods. And I will say to my soul, Soul, thou hast much goods laid up for many years; take thine ease, eat, drink, and be merry. But God said unto him, Thou fool, this night thy soul shall be required of thee: then whose shall those things be, which thou hast provided? So is he that layeth up treasure for himself, and is not rich toward God."*

This passage reminds us that worldly possessions are temporary. They do not last. Only spiritual treasures endure for eternity. The things of this world will pass away, but the things of God remain forever.

The Christian Life is Too Hard

On the contrary, it is the sinner's life that is truly difficult. The Christian life, despite its challenges, is one of peace and joy. Jesus Himself declared in *Matthew 11:30, "For my yoke is easy, and my burden is light."*

1 John 5:3 reinforces this truth: "For this is the love of God, that we keep his commandments: and his commandments are not grievous." God's commands are not burdensome but lead to abundant life. Meanwhile, Proverbs 13:15 highlights the true hardship of sin: *"Good understanding giveth favour: but the way of transgressors is hard."* Sin brings struggle and suffering, while obedience to God brings peace.

I Am Seeking Christ But Cannot Find Him

According to Jeremiah 29:13, God promises that those who seek Him wholeheartedly will find Him: *"And ye shall seek me, and find me, when ye shall search for me with all your heart."*

The Bible consistently affirms this truth. In Luke 15:1-10, Jesus illustrates God's deep love for the lost through parables of a lost sheep, a lost coin, and a lost son. These stories show that not only does God welcome seekers, but He actively pursues them with love and rejoicing when they are found.

Pastor Dr. Claudine Benjamin

Additionally, Luke 19:10 captures the very mission of Christ: *"For the Son of man is come to seek and to save that which was lost."*

If someone is truly seeking Christ, they will not seek in vain. God is already reaching out, ready to be found by those who sincerely desire Him.

Chapter 9

Ones With Excuses

Human beings often find excuses not to surrender their lives to God. Fear, uncertainty, a lack of purpose, or an unwillingness to forsake sin can all stand in the way. Yet, God's invitation remains open to all who sincerely seek Him.

Isaiah 55:7 offers a powerful assurance of God's mercy: *"Let the wicked forsake his way, and the unrighteous man his thoughts: and let him return unto the Lord, and he will have mercy upon him; and to our God, for he will abundantly pardon."*

No excuse can outweigh the grace and forgiveness God offers. Those who turn to Him will find joy and peace, even in a troubled and wicked world.

My Heart Is Too Hard

Some may feel their heart is too hardened to change, but God promises transformation. In Ezekiel 36:26-27, He assures us that no heart is beyond His power to renew: *"A new heart also will I give you, and a new spirit will I put within you: and I will take away the stony heart out of your flesh, and I will give you a heart of flesh.*

Pastor Dr. Claudine Benjamin

And I will put my spirit within you, and cause you to walk in my statutes, and ye shall keep my judgments, and do them."

This is God's promise of a complete renewal—changing a resistant heart into one that is responsive and obedient to Him. When God does this work, a person will desire His will in every area of life.

God Will Not Receive Me or I Am Afraid I Have Committed The Unpardonable Sin

Those who sincerely struggle with the fear that God will not receive them—or that they have committed the unpardonable sin—are often the most difficult to reassure.

A powerful scripture to share with them is John 6:37: *"All that the Father giveth me shall come to me; and him that cometh to me I will in no wise cast out."* This verse is a source of hope, declaring that Jesus will never reject anyone who comes to Him.

Many utterly despondent souls have found light and peace through this promise in God's Word. His unconditional, relentless love assures us that He forgives and saves—not because of who we are or what we have done, but because of the finished work of Christ.

Revelation 22:17 is another powerful scripture, showing that anyone who desires can freely receive the water of life: *"And the Spirit and the bride say, Come. And let him that heareth say, Come. And let him that is athirst come. And whosoever will, let him take the water of life freely."*

Likewise, Isaiah 55:1 is a divine invitation urging people to seek God for spiritual nourishment, which He gives freely: *"Ho, everyone that thirsteth, come ye to the waters, and he that hath no money; come ye, buy, and eat; yea, come, buy wine and milk without money and without price."*

Isaiah 1:18 reinforces the boundless mercy of God, declaring that no matter the depth of one's sins, He is willing to cleanse and forgive: *"Come now, and let us reason together, saith the Lord: though your sins be as scarlet, they shall be as white as snow; though they be red like crimson, they shall be as wool."*

Acts 10:43 and John 3:16 further emphasize the "whosoevers" of the gospel. Regardless of their past, anyone who calls upon the name of the Lord in genuine repentance can find forgiveness and eternal life. This is confirmed again in Romans 10:13: *"For whosoever shall call upon the name of the Lord shall be saved."*

Understanding the Unpardonable Sin

It is sometimes helpful to refer to Hebrews 6:4-6 and Matthew 12:31-32 to clarify what the unpardonable sin truly is and its consequences.

Matthew 12:31-32 teaches that blasphemy against the Holy Spirit is an unpardonable sin. The Holy Spirit convicts sinners, converts the repentant, and consecrates believers. Therefore, if someone speaks evil against the Holy Spirit or persistently rejects His work, they leave no room for conviction and conversion.

As Hebrews 6:4-6 reveals, the difficulty is not God's unwillingness to forgive, but man's unwillingness to believe and obey God's call to repentance. The real danger lies in a hardened heart that resists the Spirit's prompting.

However, those who are concerned about their salvation need not fear committing the unpardonable sin. A heart that seeks God is evidence that His grace is still at work. Often, a little instruction in this area is all that is needed to provide assurance.

Scripture References

Matthew 12:31-32, "Wherefore I say unto you, All manner of sin and blasphemy shall be forgiven unto men: but the blasphemy against the Holy Ghost shall not be forgiven unto men. And whosoever speaketh a word against the Son of man, it shall be forgiven him: but whosoever speaketh against the Holy Ghost, it shall not be forgiven him, neither in this world, neither in the world to come."

Hebrews 6:4-6, "For it is impossible for those who were once enlightened, and have tasted of the heavenly gift, and were made partakers of the Holy Ghost, And have tasted the good word of God, and the powers of the world to come, If they shall fall away, to renew them again unto repentance; seeing they crucify to themselves the Son of God afresh, and put him to an open shame."

"It's Too Late"

When someone says, *"It's too late for me,"* remind them of God's promise in *2 Corinthians 6:2, "(For he saith, I have heard thee in a time accepted, and in the day of salvation have I succoured thee: behold, now is the accepted time; behold, now is the day of salvation.)"*

Right now is the right time to seek the Lord—because tomorrow is never guaranteed.

The Urgency in Winning Souls

A powerful example of God's mercy is found in Luke 23:39-43. As Jesus hung on the cross, one of the criminals beside Him mocked, but the other, recognizing his guilt, turned to Jesus and said, *"Lord, remember me when thou comest into thy kingdom."* Jesus responded with a promise of salvation: *"Verily I say unto thee, Today shalt thou be with me in paradise."*

Even in his final moments, the repentant thief was saved, proving that no one is ever beyond God's grace.

Furthermore, 2 Peter 3:9 reassures us that God is patient, longing for all to repent: *"The Lord is not slack concerning his promise, as some men count slackness; but is longsuffering to us-ward, not willing that any should perish, but that all should come to repentance."*

Finally, Deuteronomy 4:30-31 offers a comforting promise: *"When thou art in tribulation, and all these things are come upon thee, even in the latter days, if thou turn to the Lord thy God, and shalt be obedient unto his voice; (For the Lord thy God is a merciful God;) he will not forsake thee, neither destroy thee, nor forget the covenant of thy fathers which he sware unto them."*

No matter how far someone has gone, as long as they have breath, **it is never too late** to come to Christ. God is merciful and always ready to receive those who turn to Him in repentance.

Chapter 10

The Self-Righteous Ones

Self-righteous people are those who entertain false hopes of salvation. Perhaps the largest group among them are those who expect to be saved by their own righteousness. They can often be recognized by statements like:

- "I am doing the best I can."
- "I do more good than bad."
- "I am not a great sinner."
- "I have never done anything very wrong."

They believe their own opinions and actions make them morally superior to others. However, the Bible makes it clear that self-righteousness is not enough for salvation.

Galatians 3:10 is a powerful verse to use in this context, as it shows that all who rely on their works are under the curse of the law: *"For as many as are of the works of the law are under the curse: for it is written, Cursed is every one that continueth not in all things which are written in the book of the law to do them."*

No one can be saved through the law unless they perfectly obey all of it—which is impossible.

Similarly, **James 2:10**, **Galatians 2:16**, and **Romans 3:19-20** reinforce this truth:

- *James 2:10, "For whosoever shall keep the whole law, and yet offend in one point, he is guilty of all."*

- *Galatians 2:16, "Knowing that a man is not justified by the works of the law, but by the faith of Jesus Christ, even we have believed in Jesus Christ, that we might be justified by the faith of Christ, and not by the works of the law: for by the works of the law shall no flesh be justified."*

- *Romans 3:19-20, "Now we know that what things soever the law saith, it saith to them who are under the law: that every mouth may be stopped, and all the world may become guilty before God. Therefore by the deeds of the law there shall no flesh be justified in his sight: for by the law is the knowledge of sin."*

These verses make it clear: No one can be justified by their own righteousness. Salvation comes only through faith in Jesus Christ. All these passages reveal the kind of righteousness that God demands. No human righteousness meets God's perfect standard. Therefore, it must be clearly understood that **salvation is based solely on God's grace through faith in Jesus Christ**—not on personal efforts to follow the law.

Another effective approach when speaking to self-righteous individuals is to emphasize that **God looks at the heart** rather than just outward actions. **Luke 16:15, Romans 2:16, and 1 Samuel 16:7** illustrate this truth:

- *Luke 16:15, "And he said unto them, Ye are they which justify yourselves before men; but God knoweth your hearts: for that which is highly esteemed among men is abomination in the sight of God."*

- *Romans 2:16, "In the day when God shall judge the secrets of men by Jesus Christ according to my gospel."*

- *1 Samuel 16:7, "But the Lord said unto Samuel, Look not on his countenance, or on the height of his stature; because I have refused him: for the Lord seeth not as man seeth; for man looketh on the outward appearance, but the Lord looketh on the heart."*

Hold your inquirer to this crucial point: **every person, when confronted with the reality that God examines the heart, must recognize their own unworthiness.** No matter how good one's outward life may seem, the heart cannot stand the perfect scrutiny of God's holy standard.

This truth leads directly to the need for **grace and salvation through Jesus Christ alone.**

No matter how self-righteous a person may be, deep within their heart lies the consciousness of sin. Our task is to labor until we reach that point. Whether they acknowledge it or not, every person's conscience testifies to the truth.

Pastor Dr. Claudine Benjamin

When someone claims, *"I'm doing the best I can"* or *"I do more good than evil,"* we must help them see their mistake. Jesus Himself declared the greatest commandment in Matthew 22:37: *"Thou shalt love the Lord thy God with all thy heart, and with all thy soul, and with all thy mind."*

This commandment requires wholehearted devotion to God—encompassing every part of our being: heart, soul, and mind. Loving God must be the central focus of our lives, surpassing all else in importance.

Salvation is not based on human effort or moral comparison but is a work of faith. Hebrews 11:6 reminds us: *"Without faith, it is impossible to please Him."*

God requires faith; without it, no one can stand righteous before Him.

John 16:8-9 highlights that unbelief in Christ is the greatest sin: *"And when he is come, he will reprove the world of sin, and of righteousness, and of judgment: Of sin, because they believe not on me."*

The Holy Spirit convicts people of sin, and here, Jesus identifies the root issue—not believing in Him. At its core, sin stems from a lack of trust in God's provision for salvation through Jesus Christ.

John 3:36 makes it clear that eternal life hinges on whether a person accepts or rejects Christ by faith: *"He that believeth on the Son hath everlasting life: and he that believeth not the Son shall not see life; but the wrath of God abideth on him."*

Likewise, Hebrews 10:28-29 reveals that the gravest offense is to trample underfoot the Son of God, rejecting His sacrifice. Before sharing this passage, you might ask, *"Do you realize that you are committing the most serious sin in God's eyes?"* Then, read the scriptures with solemnity and conviction to emphasize what God's Word says.

He that despised Moses' law died without mercy under two or three witnesses: Of how much sorer punishment, suppose ye, shall he be thought worthy, who hath trodden under foot the Son of God, and hath counted the blood of the covenant, wherewith he was sanctified, an unholy thing, and hath done despite unto the Spirit of grace? (Hebrews 10:28-29).

The Danger of Misunderstanding God's Goodness

Some believe that God is too good to judge them, but this is a false hope. If someone expresses this idea, you can respond: *"We only know of God's goodness from the Bible. Therefore, we must look to scripture to understand His character."*

Romans 2:4-5 clarifies the purpose of God's goodness: *"Or despisest thou the riches of his goodness and forbearance and longsuffering; not knowing that the goodness of God leadeth thee to repentance? But after thy hardness and impenitent heart treasurest up unto thyself wrath against the day of wrath and revelation of the righteous judgment of God."*

God's goodness is meant to lead us to repentance, not to encourage complacency in sin. Those who reject His kindness are storing up wrath for themselves. John 8:21, 24, and John 3:36 reinforce that no matter how good a person may perceive God to be, He will reject those who reject His Son.

The Human Choice to Reject Eternal Life

God desires that none should perish, offering the gift of eternal life freely. Yet, there remains one great obstacle. John 5:40 reveals what it is: *"And ye will not come to me, that ye might have life."* The problem is not a lack of opportunity but a deliberate refusal to come to Christ. People choose to remain separated from Him despite His open invitation. The sobering reality is this: life is offered, but if a person refuses it, the only alternative is eternal destruction.

The Urgency of Repentance

Scripture gives serious warnings about the necessity of repentance. 2 Peter 2:4-6, 9 and Luke 13:3 underscore that those who do not turn from sin will face judgment: *"For if God spared not the angels that sinned, but cast them down to hell, and delivered them into chains of darkness, to be reserved unto judgment; 5 And spared not the old world, but saved Noah the eighth person, a preacher of righteousness, bringing in the flood upon the world of the ungodly; 6 And turning the cities of Sodom and Gomorrha into ashes, condemned them with an overthrow, making them an ensample unto those that after should live ungodly."* (2 Peter 2:4-6)

2 Peter 2:9 offers both a warning and a promise: *"The Lord knoweth how to deliver the godly out of temptations, and to reserve the unjust unto the day of judgment to be punished."*

The Urgency in Winning Souls

These passages serve as urgent calls to repentance. God's mercy is available now, but those who persist in rejecting Him will face eternal consequences.

It is crucial to emphasize the necessity of accepting Jesus Christ as Lord and Savior because God's judgment is imminent for those who do not turn from their sins. One might say, *"God is too good to destroy anyone."* However, let us see what God Himself says in His Word. Luke 13:3 reads, *"Except ye repent, ye shall all likewise perish."* Repeating this verse multiple times can help the person grasp its serious implications.

Another group of people who entertain false hopes are those who say, *"I'm trying to be a Christian."* However, John 1:12 speaks to this: *"But as many as received him, to them gave he power to become the sons of God, even to them that believe on his name."* This shows that one does not try to be a Christian, live a better life, or earn salvation. Rather, it is about receiving Jesus Christ, who has already accomplished everything necessary for our salvation. He will continue His work of grace in our lives until the day of Jesus Christ (see Philippians 1:6).

Acts 16:31 further clarifies that God does not ask us to try what we can do but rather to trust in what Jesus has done and will continue to do: *"Believe on the Lord Jesus Christ, and thou shalt be saved."* Similarly, Romans 3:25 explains that we are not justified by our own efforts, but by freely accepting God's grace through the redemption found in Christ Jesus—on the simple condition of faith.

False Hope Based on Feelings

Another group that entertains false hope consists of those who say, *"I feel I'm going to heaven"* or *"I feel I'm saved."* However, salvation is not based on personal feelings but on the truth of God's Word.

John 3:36 makes this clear: *"He that believeth on the Son hath everlasting life: and he that believeth not the Son shall not see life; but the wrath of God abideth on him."* It is not about what one *feels* but about what God *says*.

Luke 18:18-24 presents a striking example. You can introduce this passage by saying: *"There was a man in the Bible who thought he was right with God, but in the end, he was all wrong."* This story demonstrates that true devotion to God often requires radical sacrifice and prioritizing spiritual riches over earthly wealth.

The man in this passage was sincere in seeking eternal life, but when Jesus told him to sell all he had and follow Him, he was unwilling to let go of his possessions. Tragically, nothing more is heard about this man after he walked away from Jesus. His story is a sobering reminder that an attachment to material wealth can hinder one's spiritual journey and relationship with God.

Proverbs 14:12 reinforces this truth: *"There is a way which seemeth right unto a man, but the end thereof are the ways of death."* It is of utmost importance to seek God's guidance to discern right from wrong and avoid deception.

False Hope While Living in Sin

Another group that clings to false hope consists of those claiming to be saved while living in sin. The Bible warns against such deception. Here are some key passages to help guide an individual in this situation:

- *1 Corinthians 6:9-10, "Know ye not that the unrighteous shall not inherit the kingdom of God? Be not deceived: neither fornicators, nor idolaters, nor adulterers, nor effeminate, nor abusers of themselves with mankind, nor thieves, nor covetous, nor drunkards, nor revilers, nor extortioners, shall inherit the kingdom of God."*

This passage clearly states that those who continue in sin without repentance will not inherit God's kingdom.

- *1 John 5:4-5, "For whatsoever is born of God overcometh the world: and this is the victory that overcometh the world, even our faith. Who is he that overcometh the world, but he that believeth that Jesus is the Son of God?"*

This verse highlights that those truly born of God have the power to overcome the temptations and pressures of the world. A person living in unrepentant sin, unable to overcome worldly desires, gives evidence that they have not been truly born of God.

Chapter 11

†

Skeptics

Some skeptics—those who doubt or are not easily convinced—treat the Word of God lightly. If someone dismisses the Bible as foolish, you can point them to what scripture says about this attitude.

1 Corinthians 1:18 states: *"For the preaching of the cross is to them that perish foolishness; but unto us which are saved it is the power of God."*

You can explain that some people see the gospel as foolishness because they are still lost in sin. However, the moment a person receives the Lord Jesus as their personal Savior, everything changes. A transformation takes place, and they begin to see Christ, God, and His Word in a new light.

Those who have surrendered their lives to the Lord can testify to this change. The old taste for sin fades away, replaced by a desire to walk in righteousness. This truth may be surprising to skeptics, but as the saying goes, *"He who feels it, knows it."*

Pastor Dr. Claudine Benjamin

Why Skeptics Struggle to Believe

1 Corinthians 2:14 explains why many skeptics reject the truth of God's Word: *"But the natural man receiveth not the things of the Spirit of God: for they are foolishness unto him: neither can he know them, because they are spiritually discerned."*

The reality is that a person without the Holy Spirit cannot understand or accept spiritual truths. The Holy Spirit illuminates the mind and reveals the truth of God's Word.

Additionally, 2 Corinthians 4:3-4 describes the spiritual blindness that prevents many from seeing the gospel: *"But if our gospel be hid, it is hid to them that are lost: In whom the god of this world hath blinded the minds of them which believe not, lest the light of the glorious gospel of Christ, who is the image of God, should shine unto them."*

This passage reveals that skepticism often arises because Satan, "the god of this world," has blinded unbelievers, keeping them from recognizing the truth of Christ.

2 Thessalonians 2:10-12 further explains the root of skepticism, delusion, and ultimate judgment: *"And with all deceivableness of unrighteousness in them that perish; because they received not the love of the truth, that they might be saved. And for this cause God shall send them strong delusion, that they should believe a lie: That they all might be damned who believed not the truth, but had pleasure in unrighteousness."*

This passage warns that rejecting the truth of the gospel leads to deception and, ultimately, destruction. The more a person resists God's truth, the deeper they fall into spiritual delusion.

Encouragement for Skeptics

While skepticism can be a barrier to faith, it is not impossible to reach a skeptic. If a doubter is willing to seek the truth with an open heart, God is faithful to reveal Himself. Jesus said in John 7:17: *"If any man will do his will, he shall know of the doctrine, whether it be of God, or whether I speak of myself."*

Encourage skeptics to genuinely seek God, read His Word, and ask Him to reveal the truth. The Holy Spirit is ready to open their eyes if they are willing to receive Him.

The Danger of Rejecting the Truth

If we persist in rejecting the truth of God's Word, scripture warns that God will send a "strong delusion." This means that those who refuse to accept the truth will inevitably embrace lies and falsehood, leading to their condemnation.

2 Thessalonians 2:10-12 states, *"And with all deceivableness of unrighteousness in them that perish; because they received not the love of the truth, that they might be saved. And for this cause God shall send them strong delusion, that they should believe a lie: That they all might be damned who believed not the truth, but had pleasure in unrighteousness."*

This passage serves as a sobering warning: those who reject God's truth will become increasingly deceived, believing lies that lead to eternal destruction.

The Terrible Consequences of Unbelief

Jesus Himself warned of the fate of those who refuse to believe in Him. In John 8:21-24, He declares: *"Then said Jesus again unto them, I go my way, and ye shall seek me, and shall die in your sins: whither I go, ye cannot come. Then said the Jews, Will he kill himself? because he saith, Whither I go, ye cannot come. And he said unto them, Ye are from beneath; I am from above: ye are of this world; I am not of this world. I said therefore unto you, that ye shall die in your sins: for if ye believe not that I am he, ye shall die in your sins."*

This passage highlights the severe and eternal consequences of rejecting Jesus. It is a critical choice—accepting Him as Lord leads to life but rejecting Him results in eternal separation from God.

The Root of Skepticism

John 5:44 sheds light on one of the main reasons people struggle with unbelief: *"How can ye believe, which receive honour one of another, and seek not the honour that cometh from God only?"*

Many people reject Christ because they value the approval of men more than the approval of God. Fear of rejection, pride, and societal pressures often become barriers to accepting Jesus as the true source of worth and salvation.

A Cautionary Use of Psalm 14:1

In some cases, Psalm 14:1 may be relevant, though it should be shared with great care, sincerity, and tenderness: *"The fool hath said in his heart, There is no God. They are corrupt, they have done abominable works, there is none that doeth good."*

This verse reveals that deep corruption in the heart can lead to outright denial of God. Satan desires to keep people in a state of rebellion, where they reject the truth to avoid accountability before their Creator. Those who completely deny God's existence often do so because they do not want to acknowledge His authority over their lives.

A Call to Choose Wisely

Rejecting Jesus Christ is not a trivial matter but a decision with eternal consequences. As Hebrews 3:15 urges: *"To day if ye will hear his voice, harden not your hearts."*

Skeptics must recognize that God is calling them to salvation, and ignoring His voice leads to dangerous deception. Those who truly seek the truth will find it.

Skepticism and the Authority of God's Word

Skepticism is not man's real problem—sin is. Even if a person abandons skepticism, their deeper issue remains unless they accept Jesus Christ. When a person comes to Christ, their doubts begin to resolve themselves.

Romans 3:3-4 makes it clear that questioning the truth does not change the truth: *"For what if some did not believe? Shall their unbelief make the faith of God without effect? God forbid: yea, let God be true, but every man a liar; as it is written, That thou mightest be justified in thy sayings, and mightest overcome when thou art judged."*

Another powerful verse that the Holy Spirit often uses to convict skeptics is Matthew 24:35: *"Heaven and earth shall pass away, but my words shall not pass away."* This verse reassures us of the certainty and immutability of God's Word.

Christ's Testimony of the Old and New Testaments

Some skeptics claim to accept Christ's authority while rejecting the Old Testament. However, Jesus Himself affirmed that the Old Testament is the Word of God:

- *Mark 7:13, "Making the word of God of none effect through your tradition, which ye have delivered: and many such like things do ye."*

- *Matthew 5:18, "For verily I say unto you, Till heaven and earth pass, one jot or one tittle shall in no wise pass from the law, till all be fulfilled."*

- *John 10:35, "If he called them gods, unto whom the word of God came, and the scripture cannot be broken."*

These verses show that Christ fully endorsed the Old Testament. If we accept Christ's authority, we must also accept the authority of the Old Testament.

Similarly, Jesus also confirmed the authority of the New Testament:

- *John 14:26, "But the Comforter, which is the Holy Ghost, whom the Father will send in my name, he shall teach you all things, and bring all things to your remembrance, whatsoever I have said unto you."*

- *John 16:12-13, "I have yet many things to say unto you, but ye cannot bear them now. Howbeit when he, the Spirit of truth, is come, he will guide you into all truth: for he shall not speak of himself; but whatsoever he shall hear, that shall he speak: and he will shew you things to come."*

These passages affirm that the Holy Spirit guided the apostles in writing the New Testament, ensuring its divine inspiration.

Paul's Teachings as the Word of God

Some skeptics claim that Paul never asserted his teachings as the Word of God, but 1 Thessalonians 2:13 refutes this: *"For this cause also thank we God without ceasing, because, when ye received the word of God which ye heard of us, ye received it not as the word of men, but as it is in truth, the word of God, which effectually worketh also in you that believe."*

Other passages that confirm the divine origin of Scripture include:

- *2 Peter 1:21, "For the prophecy came not in old time by the will of man: but holy men of God spake as they were moved by the Holy Ghost."*

- *John 8:47, "He that is of God heareth God's words: ye therefore hear them not, because ye are not of God."*

Pastor Dr. Claudine Benjamin

In Luke 16:30-31, Jesus emphasizes that if people do not believe God's Word, even miracles will not convince them.

The Reality of Life After Death

Every person must come to terms with the reality of life after death. The Bible clearly teaches this truth:

- *1 Corinthians 15:35-36, "But some man will say, How are the dead raised up? and with what body do they come? Thou fool, that which thou sowest is not quickened, except it die."*

- *John 5:28-29, "Marvel not at this: for the hour is coming, in the which all that are in the graves shall hear his voice, and shall come forth; they that have done good, unto the resurrection of life; and they that have done evil, unto the resurrection of damnation."*

- *Daniel 12:2, "And many of them that sleep in the dust of the earth shall awake, some to everlasting life, and some to shame and everlasting contempt."*

The Reality of Eternal Punishment

Some people doubt the doctrine of eternal punishment, but scripture is clear on this matter. Revelation 21:8 describes those who will suffer the second death: *"But the fearful, and unbelieving, and the abominable, and murderers, and whoremongers, and sorcerers, and idolaters, and all liars, shall have their part in the lake which burneth with fire and brimstone: which is the second death."*

The Urgency in Winning Souls

Revelation 17:8 and 20:10 further clarify that this punishment is eternal:

- *Revelation 17:8a, "The beast that thou sawest was, and is not; and shall ascend out of the bottomless pit, and go into perdition."*

- *Revelation 20:10, "And the devil that deceived them was cast into the lake of fire and brimstone, where the beast and the false prophet are, and shall be tormented day and night for ever and ever."*

These passages confirm that those who reject God do not simply cease to exist—they face eternal judgment.

The Book of Life and Final Judgment

- Only those whose names are written in the book of life will be saved. (see Revelation 13:7-8).

- Jesus warns of judgment after death: *"Fear him, which after he hath killed hath power to cast into hell."* (see Luke 12:5).

- The sin of blasphemy against the Holy Spirit is unforgivable and results in eternal damnation. (see Mark 3:28-29).

- Jesus warns of severe judgment: *"Good were it for that man if he had never been born."* (see Mark 14:21).

Hell is a Place of Conscious Existence

Some argue that hell is merely annihilation, but Scripture teaches otherwise:

- *2 Peter 2:4, "For if God spared not the angels that sinned, but cast them down to hell, and delivered them into chains of darkness, to be reserved unto judgment."*

- *Jude 6, "And the angels which kept not their first estate, but left their own habitation, he hath reserved in everlasting chains under darkness unto the judgment of the great day."*

Hell is not a place where people cease to exist—it is a place where they are kept alive for God's judgment.

The Critical Choice

Rejecting God's Word has eternal consequences. Skeptics may question scripture, but their doubts do not change the truth. Jesus calls each person to make a decision: *"To day if ye will hear his voice, harden not your hearts." (Hebrews 3:15)*.

Those who seek the truth with an open heart will find it, for Jesus promised: *"If any man will do his will, he shall know of the doctrine, whether it be of God…" (John 7:17)*.

The choice is clear—accept Jesus Christ and His Word or face eternal separation from God.

The Bible repeatedly warns that rejecting Jesus Christ has eternal consequences. Scripture provides clear evidence that divine judgment is real and that honoring the Son is inseparable from honoring the Father.

Hebrews 10:28-29 makes it clear that while punishment under the Mosaic Law was severe, rejecting Jesus Christ brings even greater condemnation: *"He that despised Moses' law died without mercy under two or three witnesses: Of how much sorer punishment, suppose ye, shall he be thought worthy, who hath trodden under foot the Son of God, and hath counted the blood of the covenant, wherewith he was sanctified, an unholy thing, and hath done despite unto the Spirit of grace?"*

Jesus Himself confirmed that the final judgment will be severe, as stated in Matthew 25:41: *"Then shall he say also unto them on the left hand, Depart from me, ye cursed, into everlasting fire, prepared for the devil and his angels."*

This aligns with **Revelation 9:20** and **Revelation 21:10**, which describe the ultimate fate of those who follow the beast, the false prophet, and Satan—eternal torment.

The Necessity of Honoring the Son

John 5:23b emphasizes that, *"He that honoureth not the Son honoureth not the Father which hath sent him."*

To deny Christ's divinity is to reject God Himself. 1 John 2:22-23 warns against such denial: *"Who is a liar but he that denieth that Jesus is the Christ? He is antichrist, that denieth the Father and the Son. Whosoever denieth the Son, the same hath not the Father: [but] he that acknowledgeth the Son hath the Father also."*

Faith in Jesus as the Son of God is the foundation of salvation:

- *1 John 5:1a, "Whosoever believeth that Jesus is the Christ is born of God."*

- *1 John 5:5, "Who is he that overcometh the world, but he that believeth that Jesus is the Son of God?"*

Rejecting Christ is not just disbelief—it is making God a liar. 1 John 5:10-12 states: *"He that believeth on the Son of God hath the witness in himself: he that believeth not God hath made him a liar; because he believeth not the record that God gave of his Son. And this is the record, that God hath given to us eternal life, and this life is in his Son. He that hath the Son hath life; and he that hath not the Son of God hath not life."*

This passage makes it clear that salvation and eternal life are found only in Christ.

The Eternal Consequence of Rejecting Christ

Jesus Himself warned about the fatal consequences of refusing to believe in Him:

- *John 8:24, – "I said therefore unto you, that ye shall die in your sins: for if ye believe not that I am he, ye shall die in your sins."*

Those who reject Jesus remain spiritually dead and face eternal separation from God. The only way to be saved is through faith in the divinity of Christ. As John 5:24 assures us: *"Verily, verily, I say unto you, He that heareth my word, and believeth on him that sent me, hath everlasting life, and shall not come into condemnation; but is passed from death unto life."*

The Call to Believe

The Bible presents a clear choice: believe in Jesus Christ and receive eternal life, or reject Him and face eternal separation from God. The Scriptures are unwavering in their message:

- **There is no salvation apart from Christ.**
- **Rejecting Him leads to certain judgment.**
- **Faith in Him brings eternal life.**

As Hebrews 3:15 reminds us: *"To day if ye will hear his voice, harden not your hearts."* Now is the time to believe and receive the gift of eternal life through Jesus Christ.

Chapter 12

Objections in Bringing Souls to Christ

When sharing the gospel, many people will raise objections, particularly questioning God's justice. They may argue that God is unjust or cruel. However, such accusations stem from a limited human perspective.

Questioning God's Justice

Accusing God of injustice is, in essence, challenging His authority and wisdom. The Bible directly addresses this kind of reasoning:

- Job, after questioning God, ultimately acknowledges God's infinite wisdom and repents for speaking without understanding. (see Job 42:1-6).

- **Romans 9:20** – *"Nay but, O man, who art thou that repliest against God? Shall the thing formed say to him that formed it, Why hast thou made me thus?"*

This verse in Romans is a direct rebuke to those who challenge God's authority. As creation, we are not in a position to judge the Creator.

Similarly, Romans 11:33 explains why God's ways may seem difficult to understand: *"O the depth of the riches both of the wisdom and knowledge of God! How unsearchable are his judgments, and his ways past finding out!"*

God's ways are beyond human comprehension, and His justice is perfect. The issue is not with God but with our limited understanding.

God's Discipline and Human Suffering

Some people resist coming to Christ because of their personal suffering, believing that God is unfair in allowing hardship. However, **Hebrews 12:5,7,10-11** provides an important perspective:

- *Hebrews 12:5, "And ye have forgotten the exhortation which speaketh unto you as unto children, My son, despise not thou the chastening of the Lord, nor faint when thou art rebuked of him."*

- *Hebrews 12:7, "If ye endure chastening, God dealeth with you as with sons; for what son is he whom the father chasteneth not?"*

- *Hebrews 12:10-11, "For they verily for a few days chastened us after their own pleasure; but he for our profit, that we might be partakers of his holiness. Now no chastening for the present seemeth to be joyous, but grievous: nevertheless afterward it yieldeth the peaceable fruit of righteousness unto them which are exercised thereby."*

This passage explains that suffering is often a form of discipline and refinement meant to bring people closer to God. Rather than viewing hardship as cruelty, it should be seen as an opportunity for spiritual growth.

A Call to Trust God's Wisdom

Ultimately, objections about God's justice arise from a lack of trust in His perfect plan. Scripture encourages us to surrender to God's wisdom and accept that His ways are always right.

- *Proverbs 3:5-6, "Trust in the Lord with all thine heart; and lean not unto thine own understanding. In all thy ways acknowledge him, and he shall direct thy paths."*

Instead of questioning God's ways, the real challenge is to trust Him. His justice is sure, His love is unchanging, and His desire is for all to come to repentance and salvation.

When leading souls to Christ, expect objections about God's justice. But remember:

- **God's justice is perfect** – Even if it seems beyond human comprehension.

- **Suffering has a purpose** – It can be a tool for spiritual growth and discipline.

- **Faith requires trust** – Instead of questioning God, we should seek Him with humility.

Pastor Dr. Claudine Benjamin

Encourage those who struggle with these objections to seek God's truth through His Word and trust in His divine plan.

Many people argue that God is unjust for creating men only to destroy them. However, Scripture directly refutes this claim. Ezekiel 33:11 declares: *"Say unto them, As I live, saith the Lord God, I have no pleasure in the death of the wicked; but that the wicked turn from his way and live: turn ye, turn ye from your evil ways; for why will ye die, O house of Israel?"*

This passage makes it clear—God does not take pleasure in the destruction of the wicked. Rather, He desires that they repent and live. Eternal damnation is not imposed by God's injustice but is the result of people's stubborn refusal to repent.

1 Timothy 2:3-4 further emphasizes that God does not create people just to condemn them: *"For this is good and acceptable in the sight of God our Saviour; who will have all men to be saved, and to come unto the knowledge of the truth."*

Similarly, 2 Peter 3:9 assures us: *"The Lord is not slack concerning his promise, as some men count slackness; but is longsuffering to us-ward, not willing that any should perish, but that all should come to repentance."*

The cause of man's damnation is his own willful and persistent rejection of Christ. Jesus Himself rebuked the unwillingness of people to come to Him in John 5:40: *"And ye will not come to me, that ye might have life."*

Likewise, in Matthew 23:37, He lamented over Jerusalem's rejection: *"O Jerusalem, Jerusalem, thou that killest the prophets, and stonest them which are sent unto thee, how often would I have gathered thy children together, even as a hen gathereth her chickens under her wings, and ye would not!"*

Answering Claims of Contradictions

The Bible is often criticized as being contradictory or irrational. However, Scripture explains why unbelievers perceive it this way.

1 Corinthians 1:18, "For the preaching of the cross is to them that perish foolishness; but unto us which are saved it is the power of God."

1 Corinthians 2:14, "But the natural man receiveth not the things of the Spirit of God: for they are foolishness unto him: neither can he know them, because they are spiritually discerned."

2 Corinthians 4:3-4, "But if our gospel be hid, it is hid to them that are lost: in whom the god of this world hath blinded the minds of them which believe not, lest the light of the glorious gospel of Christ, who is the image of God, should shine unto them."

Daniel 12:10 confirms that the wicked will not understand: *"Many shall be purified, and made white, and tried; but the wicked shall do wickedly: and none of the wicked shall understand; but the wise shall understand."*

For extreme cases, additional passages such as 2 Thessalonians 2:10-12, Psalm 25:14, and Matthew 11:25 shed further light.

2 Thessalonians 2:10-12 describes those who reject the truth: *"And with all deceivableness of unrighteousness in them that perish;*

because they received not the love of the truth, that they might be saved. And for this cause God shall send them strong delusion, that they should believe a lie: That they all might be damned who believed not the truth, but had pleasure in unrighteousness."

Psalm 25:14 reveals that God makes Himself known to those who fear Him: *"The secret of the Lord is with them that fear him; and he will shew them his covenant."*

Matthew 11:25 shows that God reveals truth to the humble: *"At that time Jesus answered and said, I thank thee, O Father, Lord of heaven and earth, because thou hast hid these things from the wise and prudent, and hast revealed them unto babes."*

One effective way to challenge those who claim the Bible is contradictory is to hand them a Bible and ask them to show an example. In most cases, they will not attempt to do so. Many who criticize the Bible do so without having actually read it.

Why Did Jesus Have to Die?

A common objection is: *Why did Jesus have to die? Couldn't God have saved people some other way?*

Scripture provides the answer. Isaiah 55:8-9 reminds us that God's ways are beyond human understanding: *"For my thoughts are not your thoughts, neither are your ways my ways, saith the Lord. For as the heavens are higher than the earth, so are my ways higher than your ways, and my thoughts than your thoughts."*

Romans 9:20 rebukes those who challenge God's authority: *"Nay but, O man, who art thou that repliest against God? Shall the thing formed say to him that formed it, Why hast thou made me thus?"* God, in His perfect wisdom, ordained that salvation would come through the sacrificial death of His Son. Instead of questioning why, we should be in awe of His mercy and grace.

These passages challenge people to trust God's plan rather than question His actions. He has the final authority over all things.

Often, when we urge others to accept Christ as their Savior, they respond by saying, *"There are too many hypocrites in the church."*

Romans 14:4 and 14:12 address this concern directly. These verses remind us that judging others is not our role; instead, we should focus on our own relationship with God. Verse 12 makes it clear: we will each give an account for our actions to Christ—not to other people.

Romans 2:1 further reinforces this point, warning that those who judge others are guilty of the same sins.

Now is the Time

Many people delay their decision for Christ. They say, *"I want to wait,"* *"Not tonight,"* or *"I'll think about it."*

Isaiah 55:6 urges us to: *"Seek ye the Lord while he may be found, call ye upon him while he is near:"* Similarly, Proverbs 29:1 warns of the danger of ignoring God's correction: *"He, that being often reproved hardeneth his neck, shall suddenly be destroyed, and that without remedy."*

Pastor Dr. Claudine Benjamin

Some hesitate, saying they are too young or that they will decide when they are older. Ecclesiastes 12:1 provides a clear response: *"Remember now thy Creator in the days of thy youth, while the evil days come not, nor the years draw nigh, when thou shalt say, I have no pleasure in them."*

Matthew 19:14 and 18:3 further emphasize that youth is the best time to come to Christ. Jesus Himself taught that we must become like little children to enter the kingdom of heaven.

When speaking with those who delay their decision, using the same passages that challenge indifference can be effective. The goal is to impress upon them their need for Christ so they will no longer be willing to postpone their decision.

At times, focusing on just one scripture and repeating it with conviction can be most effective. I once spoke with someone who said they couldn't decide that night. I simply quoted Psalm 29:1: *"Give unto the Lord, O ye mighty, give unto the Lord glory and strength."*

Chapter 13

†

Full of Excuses

Many people are full of excuses—willful and headstrong. They often say, *"I don't want to talk right now."* In such cases, it is often best to share a passage of Scripture and then step back, allowing God's Word to speak to their heart. Some powerful passages for this purpose include:

- *Romans 6:23, "For the wages of sin is death; but the gift of God is eternal life through Jesus Christ our Lord."*

- *Hebrews 10:28-29, "He that despised Moses' law died without mercy under two or three witnesses: Of how much sorer punishment, suppose ye, shall he be thought worthy, who hath trodden under foot the Son of God, and hath counted the blood of the covenant, wherewith he was sanctified, an unholy thing, and hath done despite unto the Spirit of grace?"*

- *Mark 16:16, "He that believeth and is baptized shall be saved; but he that believeth not shall be damned."*

- *Proverbs 29:1, "He, that being often reproved hardeneth his neck, shall suddenly be destroyed, and that without remedy."*

The Excuse of Unforgiveness

Others may protest, *"I cannot forgive someone."* But Scripture is clear that forgiveness is not optional. Matthew 6:15 warns: *"But if ye forgive not men their trespasses, neither will your Father forgive your trespasses."*

Jesus further illustrates this truth in Matthew 18:23-35, the Parable of the Unforgiving Servant, showing that those who refuse to forgive will face judgment.

Some may feel that forgiveness is impossible, but Philippians 4:13 offers reassurance: *"I can do all things through Christ which strengtheneth me."* In Ezekiel 36:26, God promises transformation: *"A new heart also will I give you, and a new spirit will I put within you: and I will take away the stony heart out of your flesh, and I will give you an heart of flesh."*

Many are kept from Christ by an unforgiving spirit. Sometimes, the key to overcoming this is simply leading them in prayer—encouraging them to kneel and ask God to remove their bitterness. Some people admit, *"I love the world too much."* Mark 8:36 is a great passage to share with them: *"For what shall it profit a man, if he shall gain the whole world, and lose his own soul?"*

Luke 12:16–20 warns against the folly of placing trust in earthly wealth. Additionally, 1 John 2:15–17 warns against loving the world, reminding us that worldly desires are fleeting. However,

Psalm 84:11 and Romans 8:32 promise that God will withhold no good thing from His children.

Excuses for Avoiding Confession

Some acknowledge their wrongdoing but hesitate to confess it. Proverbs 28:13 states: *"He that covereth his sins shall not prosper: but whoso confesseth and forsaketh them shall have mercy."*

This verse reveals the misery that follows unconfessed sin. Others might say, *"I do not want to make a public confession."* However, Romans 10:9 and Matthew 10:32–33 make it clear that confession is necessary: *"Whosoever therefore shall confess me before men, him will I confess also before my Father which is in heaven. But whosoever shall deny me before men, him will I also deny before my Father which is in heaven."*

Mark 8:38 further warns of the danger of being ashamed of Christ: *"Whosoever therefore shall be ashamed of me and of my words in this adulterous and sinful generation; of him also shall the Son of man be ashamed, when he cometh in the glory of his Father with the holy angels."*

Proverbs 24:25 reminds us that those who rebuke sin will receive blessing: *"But to them that rebuke him shall be delight, and a good blessing shall come upon them."*

Wanting One's Own Way

Some say, *"I want to have my own way."* But Isaiah 55:8–9 reminds us that God's way is far greater than ours: *"For my thoughts are not your thoughts, neither are your ways my ways, saith the Lord. For as the heavens are higher than the earth, so are my ways higher than your ways, and my thoughts than your thoughts."*

Proverbs 14:12 warns of the danger of following our own way: *"There is a way which seemeth right unto a man, but the end thereof are the ways of death."*

Refusing to Take a Stand

Some refuse to make a decision, saying, *"I neither accept Christ nor reject Him."* But Jesus leaves no room for neutrality. Matthew 12:30 states: *"He that is not with me is against me; and he that gathereth not with me scattereth abroad."*

This verse has been instrumental in convicting many.

The Church-Goer Who Trusts in Membership

Some believe they are saved simply because they attend church. A powerful way to reach such a person is to show them the necessity of the new birth. Ezekiel 36:25–27 describes this transformation, and 2 Corinthians 5:17 affirms: *"Therefore if any man be in Christ, he is a new creature: old things are passed away; behold, all things are become new."*

Likewise, 2 Peter 1:4 reminds us that being in Christ means becoming partakers of the divine nature. True salvation is not about church membership but being born again.

Many people regularly attend church and assume that "new birth" refers to baptism. However, it clearly means more than that. In *1 Corinthians 4:15*, Paul told the Galatian Christians, *"I have begotten you through the gospel."* If new birth meant baptism, Paul would have baptized them himself. Yet, in *1 Corinthians 1:14*, he declares, *"I thank God that I baptized none of you, but Crispus and Gaius."* This distinction highlights that new birth is not merely baptism but something deeper.

We see another example in *Acts 8:13–21*. Simon the Sorcerer believed and was baptized, yet later, Peter rebuked him because his heart was not right before God. This passage demonstrates that a person may be baptized while still lacking true spiritual transformation. *Acts 8:23* confirms this: *"For I perceive that thou art in the gall of bitterness, and in the bond of iniquity."* Clearly, baptism alone does not guarantee salvation; the new birth must include a genuine change of heart.

To understand what constitutes true new birth, we must examine the biblical evidence:

- *1 John 2:29, "If ye know that he is righteous, ye know that every one that doeth righteousness is born of him."*

- *1 John 5:1–4, "Whosoever believeth that Jesus is the Christ is born of God… For whatsoever is born of God overcometh the world: and this is the victory that overcometh the world, even our faith."*

These passages emphasize that new birth is characterized by faith in Christ, love for God, obedience to His commandments, and victory over sin.

How Can I Be Born Again?

The answer lies in Scripture:

- *1 John 5:12, "He that hath the Son hath life; and he that hath not the Son of God hath not life."*

- *1 Peter 1:23, "Being born again, not of corruptible seed, but of incorruptible, by the word of God, which liveth and abideth forever."*

- *James 1:18, "Of his own will begat he us with the word of truth, that we should be a kind of firstfruits of his creatures."*

New birth comes through faith in Christ and the transforming power of God's Word. It is not merely an outward ritual but an inward renewal.

The Need for Repentance

True salvation requires repentance—a turning away from sin.

- *Isaiah 55:7, "Let the wicked forsake his way, and the unrighteous man his thoughts: and let him return unto the Lord, and he will have mercy upon him."*

- *Jonah 3:10, "And God saw their works, that they turned from their evil way; and God repented of the evil, that he had said that he would do unto them; and he did it not."*

The Urgency in Winning Souls

Many churchgoers lack assurance of salvation, hoping they will be forgiven rather than knowing they are forgiven. However, Scripture assures believers of eternal life:

- *1 John 5:13, "These things have I written unto you that believe on the name of the Son of God; that ye may know that ye have eternal life."*

- *John 3:36, "He that believeth on the Son hath everlasting life: and he that believeth not the Son shall not see life; but the wrath of God abideth on him."*

Reaching Churchgoers With the Gospel

Some believe there is no point in evangelizing those who rely on church membership for salvation. However, many churchgoers are searching for something they have not found in their religious practices. If we show them the truth from God's Word, they will come to Christ and grow into strong believers.

To awaken a person to their need for salvation, we must show them their sin:

- *Matthew 22:37–38, "Jesus said unto him, Thou shalt love the Lord thy God with all thy heart, and with all thy soul, and with all thy mind. This is the first and great commandment."*

- *Isaiah 53:6, "All we like sheep have gone astray; we have turned every one to his own way; and the Lord hath laid on him the iniquity of us all."*

Pastor Dr. Claudine Benjamin

When dealing with those who are deceived, it is wise to start with *John 7:17, "If any man will do his will, he shall know of the doctrine, whether it be of God, or whether I speak of myself."* People will only come out of deception if they truly desire to know the truth. Our role is to guide them toward that desire and show them the way to Christ.

Chapter 14

✝

Soul-Winning Hints

When seeking to share the gospel, always rely on the guidance of the Holy Spirit regarding whom to approach. Generally, it is advisable to witness to those of your own sex and around your age. While the Holy Spirit may lead you to speak with someone of the opposite sex, experienced Christian workers agree that, in most cases, men are most effective in ministering to men and women to women. This is especially true for younger individuals.

Unfortunately, complications can arise when young men attempt to lead young women to Christ or vice versa. However, an elderly, motherly woman may be well-suited to minister to a young man or boy, just as an elderly, fatherly man may be effective in guiding a young woman or girl. Additionally, it is generally unwise for a young or inexperienced believer to engage in spiritual discussions with someone significantly older or more knowledgeable.

Whenever possible, share the gospel with the person privately. Most people are reluctant to open their hearts on such a personal and sacred matter when others are present. Many who would resist conviction out of pride in front of friends may acknowledge their need for Christ when spoken to one-on-one. It is typically more effective for a single worker to engage with one unconverted person at a time rather than for multiple workers to address a single inquirer. However, you may successfully lead several individuals to Christ by addressing them individually.

Depend on the Holy Spirit and the Word of God. Instead of merely quoting or reading scripture to someone, encourage them to read it for themselves. The truth can reach their heart through both their eyes and ears. It is often most effective to emphasize a single verse, repeating and discussing it until it leaves a lasting impression. Long after your conversation ends, they may still hear it ringing in their memory.

It can be powerful when someone can point to a specific verse in God's Word and say, *"I know my sins are forgiven, and I am a child of God, based on this promise."* At times, grouping together multiple passages on a particular topic can have a strong impact, convincing the mind and softening the heart.

Always keep the focus on accepting Christ. If the person tries to shift the conversation to denominational differences, baptism, theories of eternal punishment, or other secondary issues, gently guide them back to the central question: their need for a Savior. These other matters can be addressed after they have made their decision about Christ. Many opportunities for repentance have been lost because inexperienced workers allowed themselves to become distracted by side debates. Stay focused, and let the Holy Spirit do His work.

Be Courteous

Through rudeness or impertinence, many well-meaning but indiscreet Christians end up pushing away the very people they hope to lead to Christ. However, it is possible to be both honest and courteous at the same time. You can point out a person's sin without insulting them. A gentle manner allows truth to penetrate deeper because it does not stir up resistance in the heart.

Overzealous approaches can cause people to become defensive, closing themselves off in a way that makes it nearly impossible to reach them. Instead, let your kindness and sincerity create an open door for the gospel.

Be Earnest

Only an earnest Christian can truly convey the power and truth of God's Word to an unbeliever. Before using scripture to witness to others, allow those same passages to sink deeply into your own heart. Take time in prayer, kneeling before God, and meditating on His Word until you feel its power.

Paul set an example of this deep sincerity, saying: *"Therefore watch, and remember, that for three years I did not cease to warn everyone night and day with tears." (Acts 20:31).*

Genuine passion and conviction are far more effective than any training class or study book.

Never Lose Your Temper

Never let frustration take over when leading a soul to Christ. Some individuals may be exasperated, but patience and gentleness can break through even the hardest hearts. Losing your temper damages your witness and gives an unbeliever an excuse to remain in their sin.

The more irritating someone is, the more powerful your response will be if you kindly answer their insults. Often, those who are most difficult at first will later return in humility and repentance.
Avoid heated arguments at all costs. Arguments come from the flesh, not the Spirit, as Galatians 5:20 warns against: *"idolatry, sorcery, hatred, contentions, jealousies, outbursts of wrath, selfish ambitions, dissensions, heresies."*

Instead, we should reflect the fruit of the Spirit: *" love, joy, peace, longsuffering, kindness, goodness, faithfulness, gentleness, self-control. Against such there is no law." (Galatians 5:22-23)*

Arguments are often rooted in pride—the desire to "win" rather than to lead someone to Christ. If a person holds a mistaken belief that must be corrected before they can accept the gospel, address it calmly and kindly. Truth, spoken in love, is far more effective than debate.

Never Interrupt

Never interrupt someone else who is in the process of leading a soul to Christ. You may feel they are not handling it in the best way, but wait patiently—there will be opportunities for you to help later. An unskilled but sincere worker often has led someone to the brink of decision, only for another person to step in and disrupt the moment.

On the other hand, if you are the one sharing the gospel, do not let others interrupt you. A simple but kind word can prevent distractions and allow the conversation to continue smoothly.

Don't Be in a Hurry

One of the greatest weaknesses in Christian work today is haste. We often desire quick results and, in doing so, perform superficial work. Many who followed Christ came to Him slowly. Consider Nicodemus, Joseph of Arimathea, and even Peter and Paul—although Paul's final conversion seemed sudden, his transformation took time.

Paul himself spent three days in blindness and prayer after encountering Christ before making a public confession of faith: *"And now why are you waiting? Arise and be baptized, and wash away your sins, calling on the name of the Lord." (Acts 22:16).*

A single person who is carefully discipled and genuinely commits their life to Christ is far more valuable than a dozen who are rushed through a quick prayer without true understanding. It is often wise to plant a seed of truth in someone's heart and allow time for it to grow.

Jesus taught that seeds sown in shallow, rocky soil may spring up quickly but will wither just as fast. True transformation takes root in prepared hearts. Be patient, trust the Holy Spirit, and let God do His work.

The Power of Prayer in Soul-Winning

Whenever possible, ask the person you are witnessing to pray with you. Prayer has the power to break strongholds, soften hearts, and bring people into the presence of God. Many who seem resistant to the gospel have been transformed through the power of prayer.

If you encounter difficulties in soul-winning, take them to God in prayer. Ask Him for wisdom and guidance. If you struggle with using the right scriptures, study the section in this book that explains how to approach different types of people. Reflect on your experience, and, if possible, go back and try again. Even when we face apparent failures, God can use them to prepare us for greater victories.

Helping New Believers Grow

Once someone accepts Christ, it is crucial to guide them in their new faith. Without proper discipleship, many new believers struggle and fall away. The following steps will help them grow into strong followers of Christ:

1. Confess Christ Openly

Encourage new believers to publicly acknowledge their faith. Jesus calls us to confess Him before others.

- *Romans 10:9-10, "That if thou shalt confess with thy mouth the Lord Jesus, and shalt believe in thine heart that God hath raised him from the dead, thou shalt be saved. For with the heart man believeth unto righteousness; and with the mouth confession is made unto salvation."*

- *Matthew 10:32-33, "Whosoever therefore shall confess me before men, him will I confess also before my Father which is in heaven. But whosoever shall deny me before men, him will I also deny before my Father which is in heaven."*

Encourage them to share their testimony with family and friends.

2. Be Baptized and Participate in the Lord's Supper

Baptism is an outward declaration of faith and obedience to Christ. Encourage new believers to get baptized as soon as possible.

- *Acts 2:38, "Then Peter said unto them, Repent, and be baptized every one of you in the name of Jesus Christ for the remission of sins, and ye shall receive the gift of the Holy Ghost."*

Likewise, taking part in the Lord's Supper helps believers remember Christ's sacrifice.

- *Luke 22:19b, "This is my body which is given for you: this do in remembrance of me."*

3. Study the Word of God Daily

Just as physical food sustains the body, the Word of God nourishes the soul. New believers should develop the habit of reading the Bible daily.

- *1 Peter 2:2, "As newborn babes, desire the sincere milk of the word, that ye may grow thereby."*

- *Acts 20:32, " So now, brethren, I commend you to God and to the word of His grace, which is able to build you up and give you an inheritance among all those who are sanctified."*

4. Pray Daily and in Times of Temptation

A strong prayer life is essential for spiritual growth. Encourage new believers to talk to God regularly.

- *1 Thessalonians 5:17, "Pray without ceasing."*
- *Luke 11:9, "Ask, and it shall be given you; seek, and ye shall find; knock, and it shall be opened unto you."*

5. Turn Away from Sin and Walk in Obedience

Encourage them to put away sin, no matter how small, and to trust in God's guidance.

- *John 14:23, "Jesus answered and said to him, "If anyone loves Me, he will keep My word; and My Father will love him, and We will come to him and make Our home with him."*
- *Romans 14:23, "For whatsoever is not of faith is sin."*

6. Fellowship with Other Believers

Being part of a church is vital for spiritual growth. The early Christians regularly gathered for fellowship, prayer, and teaching.

The Urgency in Winning Souls

- *Hebrews 10:25, "Not forsaking the assembling of ourselves together, as the manner of some is; but exhorting one another."*
- *Acts 2:42, "And they continued steadfastly in the apostles' doctrine and fellowship, and in breaking of bread, and in prayers."*

Encourage new believers to find a Bible-teaching church where they can grow.

7. Serve Christ and Share the Gospel

New believers should be encouraged to use their talents for God's kingdom. Jesus calls us to be faithful stewards of what He has given us.

- The Parable of the Talents teaches us to invest our gifts in God's work (see Matthew 25:14-29).

Encourage them to actively share their faith with others, just as they were led to Christ.

When You Fall into Sin, Don't Give Up

Everyone stumbles at times, but God's grace is greater than our failures. Encourage believers to confess their sins immediately and continue walking with God.

- *1 John 1:9, "If we confess our sins, he is faithful and just to forgive us our sins, and to cleanse us from all unrighteousness."*

- *Philippians 3:13-14, "Brethren, I do not count myself to have apprehended; but one thing I do, forgetting those things which are behind and reaching forward to those things which are ahead, I press toward the goal for the prize of the upward call of God in Christ Jesus."*

Your Role in Follow-Up

Leading someone to Christ is just the beginning. Helping them grow is just as important. Many new believers struggle because they are not discipled properly.

- Stay in touch and encourage them.
- Pray for them daily.
- Help them stay accountable in their faith.

How to Be an Effective Witness for Christ

Jesus said, *"Follow me, and I will make you fishers of men"* (Matthew 4:19). Here's how you can be a more effective soul-winner:

1. Develop a Heart for Evangelism

Pray for God to give you a burden for the lost. Keep a list of people you are praying for and ask God for opportunities to witness to them.

2. Live a Christ-Centered Life

Your life should reflect Christ's love, integrity, and faith.

- *Matthew 5:16, "Let your light so shine before men, that they may see your good works, and glorify your Father which is in heaven."*

3. Build Genuine Relationships

Jesus often spent time with sinners, not to conform to them but to lead them to salvation. Be intentional in forming relationships with those who need Christ.

4. Memorize Key Gospel Verses

Be prepared to share the gospel by knowing key scriptures:

- *Romans 3:23, "For all have sinned, and come short of the glory of God;"*
- *Romans 6:23, "For the wages of sin is death; but the gift of God is eternal life through Jesus Christ our Lord."*
- *Romans 5:8, "But God commendeth his love toward us, in that, while we were yet sinners, Christ died for us."*
- *Romans 10:9, "That if thou shalt confess with thy mouth the Lord Jesus, and shalt believe in thine heart that God hath raised him from the dead, thou shalt be saved."*

5. Create Opportunities to Share Christ

Sometimes, you will need to take the initiative. Look for moments where you can introduce Jesus into a conversation.

6. Trust God with the Results

Pastor Dr. Claudine Benjamin

You are responsible for sharing the gospel, but only God can change hearts. Do your part, and let Him do the rest.

Chapter 15

The Uncertain

Sometimes, a lack of assurance is caused by ignorance. Scripture tells us that we may **know** we have eternal life. Often, when you ask people if they know they are saved, if their sins are forgiven, or if they have eternal life, they reply, *"Why, no one knows that."* But you can respond, *"Yes, the Bible says that all who believe may know it."*

For example, consider 1 John 5:13, *"These things have I written unto you that believe on the name of the Son of God; that ye may know that ye have eternal life, and that ye may believe on the name of the Son of God."*

Several other scriptures confirm this truth:

- *John 1:12, "But as many as received him, to them gave he power to become the sons of God, even to them that believe on his name."* This verse shows that Christ gives the power to become sons of God to all who receive Him.

Pastor Dr. Claudine Benjamin

- *John 3:36, "He that believeth on the Son hath everlasting life: and he that believeth not the Son shall not see life; but the wrath of God abideth on him."*

You can ask an inquirer, *"Who does this verse say has everlasting life?"* They will see that it is those who believe in the Son. Then ask, *"Do you believe in the Son?"* Their answer should naturally follow: *"Yes."* Then ask, *"What do you have, then?"* In a short while, their response will be: *"Everlasting life."*

Encourage them to say aloud, *"I have everlasting life,"* and then have them kneel down and thank God for giving them this gift.

Other helpful passages include:

- *John 5:24, "Verily, verily, I say unto you, He that heareth my word, and believeth on him that sent me, hath everlasting life, and shall not come into condemnation; but is passed from death unto life."*

- *1 John 5:12, "He that hath the Son hath life; and he that hath not the Son of God hath not life."*

- *Acts 13:39, "And by him all that believe are justified from all things, from which ye could not be justified by the law of Moses."*

When using Acts 13:39, ask the inquirer, *"What does the verse say about all who believe?"* When they answer correctly, *"They are justified,"* encourage them to thank God for justifying them and to confess Christ.

The Witness of the Holy Spirit

Many people struggle with assurance because they feel they do not have the witness of the Holy Spirit. However, 1 John 5:10 assures us that the testimony of God's Word is sufficient: *"He that believeth on the Son of God hath the witness in himself: he that believeth not God hath made him a liar; because he believeth not the record that God gave of his Son."*

If someone refuses to believe God's testimony, they are, in effect, calling Him a liar. Further, **Ephesians 1:13** confirms that after we believe the testimony of the Word, we are sealed with the Holy Spirit: *"In whom ye also trusted, after that ye heard the word of truth, the gospel of your salvation: in whom also after that ye believed, ye were sealed with that Holy Spirit of promise."*

The natural order of assurance is as follows:

1. **Assurance of justification** – resting on the Word of God.
2. **Public confession of Christ** – openly declaring faith.
3. **The witness of the Holy Spirit** – confirming this faith.

The problem many face is that they want to invert this order. They seek the witness of the Holy Spirit before publicly confessing Christ. However, Jesus teaches in Matthew 10:30-32: *"But the very hairs of your head are all numbered. Fear ye not therefore, ye are of more value than many sparrows. Whosoever therefore shall confess me before men, him will I confess also before my Father which is in heaven."*

Thus, we cannot expect the witness of the Spirit from the Father until Christ has confessed us before the Father. This means that the confession of Christ **must** come before the witness of the Spirit.

True and False Assurance

It is crucial to clarify what **saving faith** is. Some people claim they believe when, in reality, they do not believe **in the biblical sense**. This can lead to **false assurance** and misplaced hope.

- **John 1:12** clarifies that believing means receiving Jesus and committing oneself to Him.

- **2 Timothy 1:12** emphasizes trusting in Christ.

- **Romans 10:10** reinforces that faith is a matter of the heart: *"For with the heart man believeth unto righteousness; and with the mouth confession is made unto salvation."*

Some people who struggle with assurance may be holding on to **unconfessed sin** or engaging in **questionable practices**. These must be addressed for full assurance to come. Helpful passages include:

- *John 8:12, "Then spake Jesus again unto them, saying, I am the light of the world: he that followeth me shall not walk in darkness, but shall have the light of life."*

- *Proverbs 28:13, "He that covereth his sins shall not prosper: but whoso confesseth and forsaketh them shall have mercy."*

When sin is confessed and forsaken, and we follow Christ, we receive pardon, light, and assurance. Sometimes, it is helpful to bluntly ask, *"Is there any sin in your life that troubles your conscience?"*

Always conclude with prayer, seeking God's guidance and assurance for the inquirer.

Assurance of salvation is not based on feelings but on **God's Word, confession of Christ, and the Holy Spirit's witness**. Those who struggle with assurance must be carefully led to the truth, ensuring that they have genuinely placed their faith in Christ. Once they have, they can confidently rest in the promises of Scripture.

Summary of Key Points

1. **We can know we have eternal life** (see 1 John 5:13).
2. **Faith in Christ alone** secures salvation (see John 3:36, Acts 13:39).
3. **Assurance follows a proper order**: belief, confession, and then the witness of the Spirit (see Ephesians 1:13, Matthew 10:32).
4. **False assurance must be avoided**—true faith requires receiving Christ fully (see John 1:12, Romans 10:10).
5. **Unconfessed sin can hinder assurance**—confession and obedience lead to light and peace (see Proverbs 28:13, John 8:12).

Encourage those who struggle with assurance to **trust God's Word, confess Christ boldly**, and **walk in obedience**. True assurance will follow.

Pastor Dr. Claudine Benjamin

The Consequences of Backsliding

Backsliding is not without consequences. While God is merciful and ever willing to receive the repentant sinner, the departure from Him brings spiritual, emotional, and sometimes even physical suffering. Scripture warns repeatedly that forsaking the Lord leads to hardship, correction, and regret.

1. **The Loss of Spiritual Fulfillment**

Jeremiah 2:13 declares, *"For my people have committed two evils; they have forsaken me, the fountain of living waters, and hewed them out cisterns, broken cisterns, that can hold no water."*

To turn away from God is to abandon the source of life and nourishment. The backslider often finds that worldly pursuits, no matter how promising, ultimately fail to satisfy. They become like one who forsakes a pure, flowing fountain for a cracked, empty reservoir—left with nothing but thirst and regret.

2. **The Burden of Sin's Reproof**

Jeremiah 2:19 warns, *"Thine own wickedness shall correct thee, and thy backslidings shall reprove thee: know therefore and see that it is an evil thing and bitter, that thou hast forsaken the Lord thy God, and that my fear is not in thee, saith the Lord God of hosts."*

Sin carries its own punishment. Those who persist in backsliding eventually face its consequences—broken relationships, inner turmoil, and the weight of a guilty conscience. The pleasures of sin are fleeting, but the bitterness it leaves behind lingers.

3. Divine Discipline and Judgment

The Lord, in His righteousness, does not ignore the waywardness of His people. Amos 4:11-12 illustrates this truth: *"I have overthrown some of you, as God overthrew Sodom and Gomorrah, and ye were as a firebrand plucked out of the burning: yet have ye not returned unto me, saith the Lord. Therefore thus will I do unto thee, O Israel: and because I will do this unto thee, prepare to meet thy God, O Israel."*

God allows trials and chastisements to bring the backslider to repentance. Some may experience severe hardships as a direct result of their rebellion. This is not out of cruelty but out of divine love—just as a father disciplines his child to bring correction (see Hebrews 12:6).

4. The Danger of a Hardened Heart

One of the greatest dangers of continued backsliding is spiritual callousness. Proverbs 14:14 warns, *"The backslider in heart shall be filled with his own ways: and a good man shall be satisfied from himself."*

The longer one persists in sin, the more difficult it becomes to return. The heart that repeatedly resists the Lord's call grows cold and indifferent, eventually justifying sin rather than repenting of it. Such a state is perilous, as it leads to further alienation from God.

5. The Loss of God's Favor and Presence

1 Kings 11:9 recounts the tragic consequence of Solomon's backsliding: *"And the Lord was angry with Solomon, because his heart was turned from the Lord God of Israel, which had appeared unto him twice."*

Even the wisest man, who had seen God's presence and blessing firsthand, was not exempt from the consequences of turning away. When one forsakes the Lord, they forfeit His intimate presence and guidance. This loss is far greater than any temporary pleasure sin can offer.

The Call to Repentance and Restoration

While the consequences of backsliding are severe, the Lord, in His boundless mercy, calls the wayward to return. Scripture is filled with invitations to repentance, offering hope to those who have strayed. God does not abandon the backslider but earnestly desires their restoration.

1. The Lord's Plea for the Backslider to Return

Jeremiah 3:12-13 declares, *"Go and proclaim these words toward the north, and say, Return, thou backsliding Israel, saith the Lord; and I will not cause mine anger to fall upon you: for I am merciful, saith the Lord, and I will not keep anger forever. Only acknowledge thine iniquity, that thou hast transgressed against the Lord thy God, and hast scattered thy ways to the strangers under every green tree, and ye have not obeyed my voice, saith the Lord."*

God's first requirement is that the backslider acknowledges their sin. There can be no true restoration without genuine repentance. Yet, His promise is sure—He will not hold onto His anger forever. The Lord is not waiting to condemn but to heal.

2. The Readiness of God to Forgive

Jeremiah 3:22 further assures, *"Return, ye backsliding children, and I will heal your backslidings. Behold, we come unto thee; for thou art the Lord our God."*

No matter how far one has fallen, God stands ready to restore. He does not merely accept the backslider's return but actively heals the wounds caused by their wandering. Sin may leave scars, but divine grace is sufficient to cleanse and renew.

3. The Way Back to God

Hosea 14:1-4 provides a clear path for restoration: *"O Israel, return unto the Lord thy God; for thou hast fallen by thine iniquity. Take with you words, and turn to the Lord: say unto him, Take away all iniquity, and receive us graciously: so will we render the calves of our lips ... I will heal their backsliding, I will love them freely: for mine anger is turned away from him."*

The way back is simple yet profound—confession, prayer, and a sincere turning from sin. The backslider must recognize their fall, call upon God for mercy, and forsake their waywardness. In response, the Lord promises not only forgiveness but an outpouring of His love.

4. God's Unchanging Love and Faithfulness

Isaiah 44:22 offers one of the most beautiful assurances of restoration: *"I have blotted out, as a thick cloud, thy transgressions, and, as a cloud, thy sins: return unto me; for I have redeemed thee."*

Even when the backslider feels unworthy, God declares that He has already made provision for their redemption. His love is not fickle; His grace is not exhausted. He calls them to return, not as strangers, but as His redeemed people.

5. The Promise of a Renewed Relationship

Jeremiah 29:11-13 speaks to God's desire for reconciliation: *"For I know the thoughts that I think toward you, saith the Lord, thoughts of peace, and not of evil, to give you an expected end. Then shall ye call upon me, and ye shall go and pray unto me, and I will hearken unto you. And ye shall seek me, and find me, when ye shall search for me with all your heart."*

God's plans for the backslider have not changed. He still desires their peace and restoration. But they must seek Him wholeheartedly, casting aside all hesitations and returning in full surrender.

6. The Assurance of Cleansing

1 John 1:9 gives the final assurance to all who turn back to God: *"If we confess our sins, he is faithful and just to forgive us our sins, and to cleanse us from all unrighteousness."*

The backslider need not carry the burden of past failures. The moment they sincerely repent, God forgives and cleanses, removing every stain of unrighteousness.

A Final Appeal

The Lord's call is clear: The backslider must return. The consequences of remaining in sin are severe, but God's mercy is greater. No matter how far one has wandered, the path to restoration is open.

Let none delay in responding to this call, for as Amos 4:12 warns: *"Prepare to meet thy God, O Israel."*

Today is the day of repentance. Today is the day of restoration. Let the backslider turn back, and they will find the arms of the Savior open wide, ready to receive them once more.

Illustrations of Backsliders Who Returned to the Lord

Throughout Scripture, we see powerful examples of those who strayed from God yet found restoration through repentance. These accounts serve as encouragement to every backslider, proving that no matter how far one has fallen, the Lord stands ready to receive them with mercy and love.

1. Peter: Restored After Denial

Mark 16:7 records a remarkable moment after Christ's resurrection: *"But go your way, tell his disciples and Peter that he goeth before you into Galilee: there shall ye see him, as he said unto you."*

Peter, who had once boldly declared his unwavering loyalty to Jesus, denied Him three times when faced with pressure (see Luke 22:54-62). Overcome with sorrow, Peter wept bitterly, realizing the depth of his failure. Yet, the angel's message specifically mentioned Peter, assuring him that Jesus had not cast him away. Later, Christ personally restored Peter, reaffirming his calling (see John 21:15-19).

This example shows that even great failure does not disqualify one from God's grace. No matter how grievous the backsliding, the Lord lovingly calls His children back.

2. Israel: Restored After Seeking the Lord

2 Chronicles 15:4 testifies to God's faithfulness: *"But when they in their trouble did turn unto the Lord God of Israel, and sought him, he was found of them."*

Time and again, Israel forsook God, fell into distress, and then cried out for deliverance. Each time, when they turned back to Him with sincerity, He was found by them.

This is further illustrated in 2 Chronicles 15:12-15, where the people entered into a solemn covenant to seek the Lord with all their hearts. As a result, He granted them peace and security. This passage highlights the essential step every backslider must take: **humble confession and wholehearted return to God.**

3. The Prodigal Son: A Picture of God's Mercy

Perhaps the most powerful illustration of God's love for the repentant backslider is found in **Luke 15:11-24**, the Parable of the Prodigal Son.

A young man, eager for independence, demands his inheritance and squanders it in reckless living. When famine strikes, he is left destitute, forced to feed swine—an ultimate disgrace for a Jew. In his lowest moment, he realizes the goodness of his father and determines to return, acknowledging his unworthiness.

Yet before he can even reach home, his father sees him from afar, runs to him, embraces him, and restores him fully, rejoicing in his return.

This parable illustrates not only the **steps of repentance**—acknowledging sin, turning back, and confessing—but also **the incredible reception the repentant receives.** The father did not hesitate or punish the son; rather, he clothed him, fed him, and celebrated his return.

In the same way, God is eager to restore every backslider who comes back in humility.

The Steps to Restoration

Scripture clearly outlines the process by which a backslider may return and be restored to God's favor.

Pastor Dr. Claudine Benjamin

1. Confession of Sin

"If we confess our sins, he is faithful and just to forgive us our sins, and to cleanse us from all unrighteousness." (1 John 1:9).

A backslider must acknowledge their wrongdoing before God. True repentance requires humility and honesty.

2. Turning from Sin

"Return, thou backsliding Israel, saith the Lord; and I will not cause mine anger to fall upon you: for I am merciful, saith the Lord, and I will not keep anger forever. Only acknowledge thine iniquity..." (Jeremiah 3:12-13).

Repentance is not merely feeling sorrowful but involves forsaking sinful ways and returning fully to God.

3. Seeking the Lord Wholeheartedly

"And all Judah rejoiced at the oath: for they had sworn with all their heart, and sought him with their whole desire; and he was found of them: and the Lord gave them rest round about." (2 Chronicles 15:15).

God does not accept half-hearted repentance. The backslider must seek Him with full devotion, surrendering completely.

4. Resting in God's Forgiveness

"I have blotted out, as a thick cloud, thy transgressions, and, as a cloud, thy sins: return unto me; for I have redeemed thee." (Isaiah

44:22).

The enemy may seek to burden the repentant with guilt, but God assures complete forgiveness. Once a backslider has returned, they are **fully restored** in His grace.

Preventing Future Backsliding

Restoration is not the end of the journey. A backslider who has returned must now be strengthened in their faith to avoid falling again. Scripture provides clear guidance on maintaining a steadfast walk with God.

1. Abide in God's Word

"Thy word have I hid in mine heart, that I might not sin against thee." (Psalm 119:11).

Regular meditation on Scripture strengthens believers, equipping them against temptation and deception. A daily commitment to God's Word ensures spiritual nourishment and stability.

2. Maintain a Strong Prayer Life

"Watch and pray, that ye enter not into temptation: the spirit indeed is willing, but the flesh is weak." (Matthew 26:41).

Prayer deepens one's relationship with God and keeps the heart vigilant against spiritual decline. A consistent prayer life fosters dependence on the Lord and sensitivity to His leading.

3. Stay in Fellowship with Other Believers

"Not forsaking the assembling of ourselves together, as the manner of some is; but exhorting one another: and so much the more, as ye see the day approaching." (Hebrews 10:25).

Isolation weakens faith, while godly fellowship provides encouragement and accountability. A backslider must remain connected to the body of Christ to grow and be strengthened.

4. Walk in Obedience to the Spirit

"This I say then, Walk in the Spirit, and ye shall not fulfil the lust of the flesh." (Galatians 5:16).

Living in submission to the Holy Spirit empowers a believer to resist sin and pursue righteousness. It is through His guidance that one can maintain a life of victory.

The examples of Peter, Israel, and the Prodigal Son reveal the depths of God's mercy toward backsliders. **No matter how far one has strayed, restoration is always possible through sincere repentance.** Yet, returning to God is only the beginning—remaining faithful requires daily dependence on Him.

For every backslider, the message is clear: **God still calls you, loves you, and desires your full restoration. Return to Him today, and He will receive you with open arms.**

Chapter 16

Power for Soul-Winning

One essential condition for successful soul-winning is the empowerment of the Holy Spirit. In *Acts 1:5*, Jesus said, *"For John truly baptized with water; but ye shall be baptized with the Holy Ghost not many days hence."* Similarly, in *Luke 24:49*, He instructed His disciples: *"And, behold, I send the promise of my Father upon you: but tarry ye in the city of Jerusalem, until ye be endued with power from on high."*

In these passages, we find three key expressions: *baptized with the Holy Spirit*, *endued with power from on high*, and *filled with the Holy Spirit*. Through careful comparison of these and other related scriptures, we see that all these expressions refer to the same experience—an experience that is absolutely necessary for acceptable and effective service in Christ's kingdom.

The Baptism of the Holy Spirit: A Distinct Experience

The infilling of the Holy Spirit is a definite and distinct experience. A believer will know whether or not they have received the Holy Spirit. Jesus commanded His disciples to wait in Jerusalem until they received power from on high *(see Luke 24:49)*. If this experience were vague or uncertain, the disciples would not have known whether they had complied with Christ's command.

Moreover, the baptism of the Holy Spirit is separate from His regenerating work. In *Acts 1:5*, Jesus told His disciples that they would be baptized with the Holy Spirit not many days hence. In *Acts 8:15-16*, we read of believers who had accepted Christ and were baptized in water, yet had not received the Holy Spirit: *"Who, when they were come down, prayed for them, that they might receive the Holy Ghost: (For as yet he was fallen upon none of them: only they were baptized in the name of the Lord Jesus.)"*

Again, in *Acts 19:1-6*, Paul encountered disciples in Ephesus who had believed but had not received the Holy Spirit. When Paul laid hands on them, the Holy Spirit came upon them, and they spoke in tongues and prophesied.

Regeneration versus the Baptism of the Holy Spirit

A believer may be regenerated by the Holy Spirit without being baptized in the Holy Spirit. Such a believer is saved but not yet equipped for service. While every believer has the Holy Spirit dwelling in them *(see Romans 8:9)*, not every believer has received the baptism of the Holy Spirit.

In *Acts 8:12-16*, believers in Samaria had accepted the gospel and were baptized in water, but they had not yet received the Holy Spirit. The apostles sent Peter and John to pray for them so that they might receive this essential baptism. This demonstrates that baptism in the Holy Spirit is available to all who have been born again.

The Purpose of the Baptism of the Holy Spirit

The baptism of the Holy Spirit is always connected to testimony and service. *1 Corinthians 12:13-14 states: "For by one Spirit are we all baptized into one body, whether we be Jews or Gentiles, whether we be bond or free; and have been all made to drink into one Spirit. For the body is not one member, but many."*

This baptism is not primarily for personal purification from sin. Some mistakenly believe that receiving the Holy Spirit eradicates the carnal nature, but no scripture supports this position. Instead, the baptism of the Holy Spirit equips believers with power for ministry and service. While it often leads to greater spiritual surrender, its chief purpose is to empower believers to be effective witnesses.

Manifestations of the Holy Spirit's Baptism

To better understand the baptism of the Holy Spirit, we must examine its manifestations as recorded in scripture. *1 Corinthians 12:4-11* describes the diversity of spiritual gifts given by the Holy Spirit: *"Now there are diversities of gifts, but the same Spirit... For to one is given by the Spirit the word of wisdom; to another the word of knowledge... To another faith... To another the gifts of healing... To another the working of miracles... To another prophecy... To another discerning of spirits... To another divers kinds of tongues... But all these worketh that one and the selfsame Spirit, dividing to every man severally as he will."*

The results of Holy Spirit baptism are not identical for every believer. Not all will become evangelists or teachers; different gifts are imparted according to God's calling. Some receive the gift of teaching, others the gift of healing, and others the gift of helps *(see 1 Corinthians 12:7-11).*

Unfortunately, many fail to recognize this truth, leading to unnecessary doubt and disappointment. Instead of seeking a specific gift, believers must submit to the Holy Spirit's leading and allow Him to determine their role in God's service.

The Power and Boldness of the Holy Spirit

The baptism of the Holy Spirit imparts power for the service to which God calls each believer. It also grants boldness in testimony and ministry. In *Acts 4:29-31*, we read how the early believers prayed for boldness, and the Holy Spirit filled them, enabling them to proclaim God's Word with courage.

Compare Peter's transformation before and after receiving the Holy Spirit. In *Mark 14:66-72*, he denied Jesus three times out of fear. Yet after Pentecost, in *Acts 2*, the same Peter preached with boldness, leading thousands to salvation.

Perhaps you desire to witness for Christ but struggle with fear and timidity. If you receive the baptism of the Holy Spirit, you will find that all your hesitation and fear will be overcome.

Defining the Baptism of the Holy Spirit

The baptism of the Holy Spirit is the Spirit of God falling upon a believer, taking possession of their faculties, and imparting spiritual gifts that equip them for divine service. It is not merely an emotional experience but a supernatural equipping for ministry.

Who Needs the Baptism of the Holy Spirit?

In *Luke 24:49*, Jesus commanded His disciples to remain in Jerusalem until they were filled with power from on high. These men were eyewitnesses to Jesus' life, death, and resurrection. They had been personally trained by the Lord for over three years. Yet, despite their knowledge and experience, Jesus did not permit them to begin their ministry until they were baptized with the Holy Spirit.

If these well-trained disciples were required to wait for the Holy Spirit's power before ministering, how much more do we need this divine empowerment today? Even Jesus Himself did not begin His public ministry until He was anointed with the Holy Spirit and power *(see Acts 10:38)*.

The baptism of the Holy Spirit is an essential preparation for Christian service. Attempting to serve Christ without it is an act of presumption and ignorance of God's requirements.

The Promise of the Holy Spirit is for All Believers

It is the privilege of every believer to receive the baptism of the Holy Spirit. As *Acts 2:39* declares: *"For the promise is unto you, and to your children, and to all that are afar off, even as many as the Lord our God shall call."*

This promise is for every generation of believers. If we lack the baptism of the Holy Spirit, it is not because God has withheld it but because we have not sought it. Each believer is responsible before God for the work they could have accomplished if they had received this divine empowerment.

Pastor Dr. Claudine Benjamin

May we all seek the fullness of the Holy Spirit so we may be equipped to fulfill the great commission, bringing souls into the kingdom of God with power and boldness.

Chapter 17

✝

The Indifferent

In the work of evangelism, one will frequently encounter people who are indifferent to the gospel. These individuals may not be openly hostile to Christianity, yet they display a troubling lack of concern for their spiritual condition. They may be preoccupied with the distractions of life, skeptical about faith, or simply unwilling to think deeply about matters of eternity.

Dealing with the indifferent requires patience, wisdom, and the guidance of the Holy Spirit. The goal is to awaken their awareness of sin, point them to Christ, and warn them of the dire consequences of remaining indifferent to the truth. There are several effective approaches to reaching such individuals.

Showing Them Their Need for a Savior

One of the most effective ways to deal with an indifferent person is to show them their need for salvation. Many people assume that because they live a relatively moral life, they have no need for a Savior. However, the Bible makes it clear that all have sinned and fallen short of God's standard. **Romans 3:23** states: *"For all have sinned, and come short of the glory of God."* This verse removes any illusion of self-righteousness. No one is exempt. Every person has sinned in thought, word, or deed. Even those who consider themselves "good" are still guilty before a holy God.

Another powerful verse to use is **Isaiah 53:6**: *"All we like sheep have gone astray; we have turned every one to his own way; and the Lord hath laid on him the iniquity of us all."*

A good strategy when using this verse is to ask the person directly: *"Who has gone astray?"* If they answer honestly, they will have to admit that they too have wandered from God. Leading them to this acknowledgment is an important step in overcoming their indifference.

Confronting Their Lack of Love for God

A common reason for indifference toward the gospel is a lack of love for God. People may claim to respect God but live their lives without any real devotion to Him. Jesus addressed this in **Matthew 22:37-38** when He declared: *"Thou shalt love the Lord thy God with all thy heart, and with all thy soul, and with all thy mind. This is the first and great commandment."*

When an indifferent person hears this verse, they may realize that their heart is far from God. Asking them simple questions such as *"Do you love God with all your heart?"* or *"Do you seek to honor Him in your daily life?"* can expose their spiritual complacency.

Additionally, **Isaiah 57:21** warns: *"There is no peace, saith my God, to the wicked."*

Many indifferent people assume they are safe because they feel no immediate urgency. But this verse reveals the truth—*without God, there is no real peace.* Even if they ignore spiritual matters, their soul remains in peril.

Pointing Them to the Penalties of Sin

One of the most sobering realities of scripture is the warning that sin carries severe consequences. Many indifferent individuals fail to take this seriously, assuming that God will overlook their complacency. However, the Bible is clear that those who ignore the gospel will face judgment.

A particularly striking passage is **2 Thessalonians 1:7-9**: *"And to you who are troubled rest with us, when the Lord Jesus shall be revealed from heaven with his mighty angels, in flaming fire taking vengeance on them that know not God, and that obey not the gospel of our Lord Jesus Christ: Who shall be punished with everlasting destruction from the presence of the Lord, and from the glory of his power."*

This passage leaves no room for misunderstanding. Those who remain indifferent to Christ will one day stand before Him as Judge. The penalty for rejecting Him is everlasting destruction—eternal separation from His presence.

Similarly, **Revelation 20:15** states: *"And whosoever was not found written in the book of life was cast into the lake of fire."*

These warnings should be read with deep earnestness. The goal is not to instill fear for fear's sake but to awaken the listener to the seriousness of their condition.

Pastor Dr. Claudine Benjamin

Demonstrating Christ's Sacrifice

While it is crucial to warn the indifferent of judgment, it is equally important to show them the love of Christ. Many people remain indifferent simply because they do not truly understand what Jesus has done for them.

Isaiah 53:5-6 is a powerful passage that reveals the depth of Christ's suffering for humanity: *"But he was wounded for our transgressions, he was bruised for our iniquities: the chastisement of our peace was upon him; and with his stripes we are healed. All we like sheep have gone astray; we have turned every one to his own way; and the Lord hath laid on him the iniquity of us all."*

When sharing this passage, emphasize that Christ did not suffer for His own sins—He suffered for **our** sins. He was bruised, beaten, and crucified so that we might be redeemed. A person who remains indifferent after hearing this has not yet grasped the gravity of Christ's sacrifice.

Another compelling passage is **Hebrews 10:28-29**: *"He that despised Moses' law died without mercy under two or three witnesses: Of how much sorer punishment, suppose ye, shall he be thought worthy, who hath trodden under foot the Son of God, and hath counted the blood of the covenant, wherewith he was sanctified, an unholy thing, and hath done despite unto the Spirit of grace?"*

This verse shows that rejecting Christ is not a minor issue—it is the greatest sin of all.

John 3:18-19 reinforces this truth: *"He that believeth on him is not condemned: but he that believeth not is condemned already, because he hath not believed in the name of the only begotten Son of God. And this is the condemnation, that light is come into the world, and men loved darkness rather than light, because their deeds were evil."*

An indifferent person may not see themselves as evil, but this passage makes it clear that rejecting Christ is an act of rebellion against the light.

Trusting in God's Power

Not everyone will be willing to engage in a discussion about their spiritual state. Some will resist or avoid such conversations entirely. When this happens, it is essential to trust in the power of God rather than relying on human efforts.

If someone is unwilling to listen, the only recourse is to seek God's guidance. Pray earnestly for the Spirit of God to work in their heart, convicting them of sin and drawing them to the truth.

The scriptures provided above can be used effectively with those who are indifferent or careless. However, it is ultimately the work of the Holy Spirit to soften hearts and bring conviction. Through patience, prayer, and a reliance on God's Word, even the most indifferent soul can be awakened to the truth of salvation.

Chapter 18

The Great Commission

The Mission of Jesus and the Great Commission

Jesus was sent by the Father on a divine mission. He openly declared this truth throughout His ministry: *"For God did not send His Son into the world to condemn the world; but that the world through Him might be saved." (John 3:17).*

"Verily, verily, I say unto you, He that heareth my word, and believeth on him that sent me, hath everlasting life, and shall not come into condemnation; but is passed from death unto life." (John 5:24).

Other references confirm this mission (see John 5:36, John 6:38-40, 57, John 7:28-29, John 17:3). But the fact of His sending raises an essential question—**Why was Jesus sent?**

Jesus Himself answered: *"My food is to do the will of Him who sent Me, and to finish His work." (John 4:34 - NKJV).*

Pastor Dr. Claudine Benjamin

What is the Father's Work?

To understand the Father's work, we must distinguish between two key terms in John's Gospel: **"work"** and **"works."**

- **"Works"** refer to Jesus' individual acts—His healings, miracles, and other supernatural deeds.

- **"Work"** refers to the ultimate purpose for which He was sent—the mission of salvation.

When Jesus said He came to *finish the Father's work* (see John 4:34), He was speaking of His divine mission to redeem humanity. This work was completed at the cross when He declared, *"It is finished!"* (see John 19:30).

The Only Commission

Before His dramatic ascension into heaven, Jesus entrusted His mission to His disciples—not once, but **five times**:

- *"Go ye therefore, and teach all nations, baptizing them in the name of the Father, and of the Son, and of the Holy Ghost: Teaching them to observe all things whatsoever I have commanded you: and, lo, I am with you always, even unto the end of the world. Amen."* (Matthew 28:19-20).

- *"Go into all the world and preach the gospel to every creature." (Mark 16:15).*

- Repentance and remission of sins should be preached in His name to all nations. (see Luke 24:46-48).

- *"Then said Jesus to them again, Peace be unto you: as my Father hath sent me, even so send I you." (John 20:21).*

- *"But ye shall receive power, after that the Holy Ghost is come upon you: and ye shall be witnesses unto me both in Jerusalem, and in all Judaea, and in Samaria, and unto the uttermost part of the earth." (Acts 1:8).*

Though we often call this the **Great Commission**, it is, in reality, **the Only Commission.**

People are dying. The divine mandate was signed in blood—dripping from Christ's face in Gethsemane, trickling down His thorn-pierced brow in Pilate's hall, and pouring from His wounded side on Calvary. The command of the earth's Great Physician remains unchanged: **"Go. Preach. Baptize. Disciple. Teach."**

Beyond Salvation: The Full Mission of the Church

While saving souls is the urgent priority of the Great Commission, the mission does not stop at conversion. Jesus' command to *"make disciples of all nations"* extends beyond the moment of salvation. The church must dedicate itself to **baptizing, discipling, and maturing believers** in their faith.

Discipleship is a lifelong process. The mission of the church does not end when a sinner repents—it continues in the days, weeks, months, and years that follow. If the church fails to disciple, we leave spiritual newborns vulnerable to the same world from which they were rescued.

Pastor Dr. Claudine Benjamin

Our mission must be as focused and passionate as a team of skilled medical professionals. Pastors, volunteers, administrators, teachers, evangelists, and theologians must all recognize that their individual roles are eternally significant, **only if they connect to Christ's mission.**

Without mission, what is the point?

Without mission, all you have is:

- **A means with no end.**
- **A trip with no destination.**
- **Action without direction.**
- **Motion without meaning.**

10 Reasons the Church Must Prioritize the Great Commission

At this critical moment in history, the church must fully commit to its missional mandate. Any one of the following reasons is sufficient to call us to action, but together, they should ignite an unwavering passion.

1. The Believers' Judgment

Paul delivered a sobering reminder to the Corinthian church: *"Wherefore we labour, that, whether present or absent, we may be accepted of him. For we must all appear before the judgment seat of Christ; that every one may receive the things done in his body, according to that he hath done, whether it be good or bad. Knowing therefore the terror of the Lord, we persuade men; but we are made manifest unto God; and I trust also are made manifest in your consciences." (2 Corinthians 5:9-11).*

The judgment seat of Christ is not for unbelievers—it is for believers. This is where **our works will be tested** and our faithfulness evaluated. *What will matter on that day?* Not our titles, achievements, or earthly status but **our obedience to the mission of Christ.**

More reasons will follow, but this alone should stir our hearts.

Have We Obeyed the Great Commission?

At times, believers seem to forget that we too will stand before **the judgment seat of Christ**. The apostle Paul himself spoke of *"the terror of the Lord"* (see 2 Corinthians 5:11). In Revelation 1:14-15, John beheld the glorified Son of Man, describing His eyes *"as a flame of fire"* and His feet *"like unto fine brass, as if they burned in a furnace."* Overwhelmed by this vision, John declared in Revelation 1:17, *"And when I saw him, I fell at his feet as dead."*

Paul's words serve as a sobering reminder: *"For we must all appear before the judgment seat of Christ" (2 Corinthians 5:10).* This judgment is not to determine our eternal destiny—that was settled when we repented of our sins and received Jesus Christ as Lord. We acknowledged, like Isaiah, *"But we are all as an unclean thing, and all our righteousnesses are as filthy rags" (Isaiah 64:6a).* We accepted Christ's sacrifice as the atonement for our sins, believing that *"he hath made him to be sin for us, who knew no sin; that we might be made the righteousness of God in him" (2 Corinthians 5:21).*

Pastor Dr. Claudine Benjamin

Our faith in Christ secures our eternity. However, the **believers' judgment** is a compelling reason to remain focused on the true mission of the church. We must not become distracted by **secondary concerns**—whether the type of garments we wear or the external structures of our spiritual "health care system." Instead, we must fine-tune our vision for **saving the lost and making disciples**. There is nothing inherently wrong with large congregations, well-furnished church buildings, or polished sermons. These can reflect a natural pursuit of excellence. However, if they become **the primary reason** for the church's existence—if pastors lead and believers serve for these alone—then at the judgment seat of Christ, much of their work will be revealed as *wood, hay, and stubble, consumed by fire (see 1 Corinthians 3:12-15)*.

The church must never lose sight of its **greatest priority**: the salvation of souls and the discipleship of believers.

2. Eternal Hell

A question could be asked in many churches today—*Whatever happened to hell? Is hell real? Does the Bible mean what it says? Do people truly go there?*

Jesus spoke plainly about hell: *"And I say unto you my friends, Be not afraid of them that kill the body, and after that have no more that they can do. But I will forewarn you whom ye shall fear: Fear him, which after he hath killed hath power to cast into hell; yea, I say unto you, Fear him." (Luke 12:4–5)*.

Jesus spoke about hell more than any other person in scripture. His passionate desire to save the lost from eternal torment is evident throughout the Gospels. Some argue that the story Jesus told in

The Urgency in Winning Souls

Luke 16 is "merely a parable," but the text suggests otherwise. Jesus began with the words: *"There was a certain rich man."* This phrase strongly implies He was describing a historical person. The story must be told: *"And in hell he lift up his eyes, being in torments, and seeth Abraham afar off, and Lazarus in his bosom." (Luke 16:23)*.

The reality of hell is a compelling reason for the church to stay focused on its mission. Jesus described hell as an awful place: *"Then shall he say also unto them on the left hand, Depart from me, ye cursed, into everlasting fire, prepared for the devil and his angels:" (Matthew 25:41)*.

May God grant our generation a fresh revelation of the reality of hell. May we not shrink back for fear of being labeled politically incorrect but instead proclaim the truth about the torments of the devil's hell.

Only the church has the message that rescues people from this fate. We must preach the gospel boldly, for it alone offers the way of escape. Hell is not a place where anyone is predestined to go—salvation through Christ is available to all. But the truth of hell must be told, for only in its light can we fully grasp the urgency of the gospel.

3. **Lost People**

Some refer to Luke 15 as *"the chapter of the lost."* I prefer to call it *"the chapter of the found."* But perhaps the most accurate description is *"the chapter of the lost and found."*

Pastor Dr. Claudine Benjamin

The Pharisees and scribes were murmuring because Jesus ate with sinners—something they would never dare to do. In response, Jesus told three stories. The first is explicitly called a parable, while the other two are presented as historical events. They are commonly known as the parables of the lost sheep, the lost coin, and the lost son. But in all three, the lost was found, and those who witnessed it rejoiced. When the lost was found, transformation followed.

Dr. Gene Rice once asked, *"Can anything be worse than being lost?"* His answer: *"Yes! It's when you are lost, and no one is looking."* I would add—not only when no one is looking, but when no one cares. Lost people matter to Jesus.

One of the most striking themes of Luke 15 is the overwhelming joy when the lost are found. Each story concludes with a celebration. Heaven itself rejoices when a sinner repents. Bill Hybels said this: *"When a sinner is saved, heaven throws a party."* That joy alone should compel us to fulfill the church's missional mandate. But when the church loses its focus on seeking the lost, its joy fades.

On the other hand, history and testimonies confirm that the greatest joy in the church comes when lost souls come to Christ. Just as the birth of a child brings excitement to an earthly family, the new birth of a soul stirs rejoicing in the church family. May the joy of finding the lost—the lost sheep, the lost coin, the lost son—renew our passion for the mission.

Jesus likened the church's mission to harvesting a field: *"Behold, I say unto you, Lift up your eyes, and look on the fields; for they are white already to harvest"* (John 4:35b).

The harvest is not measured by the grain stored in the barn but by the wheat still standing in the field. There is no second chance to reap a ripened harvest. Yet, too often, we focus on the barn instead of the field. And as we wait, the grain rots.

May the Spirit of the Lord stir the church to go, reap, and keep the harvest.

4. Pentecostal Priority

Before His ascension, Jesus plainly told His disciples: *"For John truly baptized with water; but ye shall be baptized with the Holy Ghost not many days hence." (Acts 1:5).*

He then declared: *"But ye shall receive power, after that the Holy Ghost is come upon you: and ye shall be witnesses unto me both in Jerusalem, and in all Judaea, and in Samaria, and unto the uttermost part of the earth." (Acts 1:8).*

Some pentecostals emphasize *speaking in tongues* as the priority of Pentecost. The Church of God and most traditional pentecostal movements rightly teach that speaking in tongues is the initial evidence of the baptism in the Holy Spirit. However, the true priority of pentecost is what Jesus Himself emphasized: *"You shall receive power. You shall be witnesses to Me."*

The gift of pentecost is **power**. The proof of power is **witness**. And the person of witness is **Jesus Christ the Lord.**

The Holy Spirit's power is given so that every believer can be a witness—a living testimony that Jesus of Nazareth is the Son of

Pastor Dr. Claudine Benjamin

God, who died on the cross for the forgiveness of sins and the salvation of all who believe. Speaking in tongues remains, as it was on the day of Pentecost, the initial evidence of the baptism in the Holy Spirit. But the ultimate evidence is found in Acts 1:8—bold, Spirit-empowered witness. The immediate result of the 120 being filled in the upper room was not just tongues but testimony. They went into the streets of Jerusalem, proclaiming the gospel to people from all over the world.

"Then they that gladly received his word were baptized: and the same day there were added unto them about three thousand souls." (Acts 2:41).

It is easy for pentecostal churches to put the Holy Spirit in a box.

- **The "Box of the Temple"**—where He only moves within the church building.

- **The "Box of Time"**—where He must operate within a strict timeframe, usually one hour on Sunday morning.

- **The "Box of Tongues"**—where His voice is only recognized through an unknown tongue and interpretation.

- **The "Box of Tradition"**—where He is free to move, but only in ways that fit within the customs of the church, community or culture.

Jesus did not pray for the Father to send the Holy Spirit just for Him to be placed in a box. The Spirit was sent to empower believers to be witnessing, discipling missionaries. May we never restrict His work, but instead yield to His leading so that the gospel is proclaimed in power to the ends of the earth.

5. Christ's Love

No one in the New Testament was more mission-minded than the apostle Paul. Yet, despite his devotion, many in the Corinthian church criticized him—even questioning his right to be called an apostle. But Paul's greatest defense of his ministry was summed up in these simple yet profound words: *"The love of Christ constraineth us" (2 Corinthians 5:14a).*

A few verses later, Paul explained that love in terms of the church's mission: *"Therefore, if anyone is in Christ, he is a new creation; old things have passed away; behold, all things have become new. Now all things are of God, who has reconciled us to Himself through Jesus Christ, and has given us the ministry of reconciliation, that is, that God was in Christ reconciling the world to Himself, not imputing their trespasses to them, and has committed to us the word of reconciliation. Therefore, we are ambassadors for Christ, as though God were pleading through us: we implore you on Christ's behalf, be reconciled to God. For He made Him who knew no sin to be sin for us, that we might become the righteousness of God in Him." (2 Corinthians 5:17–21).*

In everyday life, love is a powerful, compelling force. If anyone doubts this truth, they need only observe the sacrifices parents willingly make for their children. Love is the greatest motivating force known to humanity. This is the very nature of God. Love was the reason He sent His Son to die for the sins of the world.

"We love Him, because he first loved us." (1 John 4:19).

Pastor Dr. Claudine Benjamin

Because of this, the love of Christ must be the driving force behind the church's mission. We witness of Him because we love Him. We serve Him because we love Him. We obey His command to engage in the greatest mission known to heaven and earth—because we love Him.

Let it never be said that the Church of God simply *designed a program, planned a strategy,* or *passed a resolution* to compel its members to take part in the mission. While such tools may serve a purpose, they must never replace the true motivation. Let it always be known that: *"The love of Christ compels us" (see 2 Corinthians 5:14).*

Dr. Raymond F. Culpepper

The Great Commission Connection

Chapter 19

Commanded to Preach: Biblical Preaching and the Great Commission

Among the parting words of our Lord Jesus Christ prior to His ascension was the command to preach the gospel. Specifically, He directed that repentance and the forgiveness of sins "be proclaimed in His name to all nations, beginning from Jerusalem" (see Luke 24:47).[1] In response, Mark records, *"And they went out and preached everywhere, while the Lord worked with them, and confirmed the word by the signs that followed." (Mark 16:20)*. One cannot read the New Testament without recognizing the prominence of preaching. More than 115 times the words translated for *preaching* appear with the principle words such as *kerusso* "to herald" (as a royal proclamation), and *euangelizo* "to announce the good news" occurring more than fifty times each.

---

[1] Unless otherwise indicated, all Scriptural references in this chapter are from the New American Standard Bible (NASB).

Pastor Dr. Claudine Benjamin

When it came to fulfilling the Great Commission, *"And every day, in the temple and from house to house, they did not stop teaching and preaching the good news of Jesus as the Christ." (Acts 5:42).*

John preached the baptism of repentance (see Acts 10:37). Phillip preached Christ at Samaria (see Acts 8:5). Peter said Jesus *"ordered us to preach to the people, and to testify solemnly that this is the One who has been appointed by God as Judge of the living and the dead." (Acts 10:42).* Paul said he was ordained and appointed to be a preacher (see 1 Timothy 2:7; 2 Timothy 1:11) and believed all other duties to be subordinate to that one divine call (see 1 Corinthians 1:17). Timothy was instructed to *"Preach the word ... in season and out of season"* (see 2 Timothy 4:2), and Peter advised those who were scattered and living as aliens to *"sanctify Christ as Lord in your hearts, always being ready to make a defense to everyone who asks you to give an account for the hope that is in you" (1 Peter 3:15).* Believers in the New Testament could not but preach, lest they deny their own identity and abdicate their ordained purpose. Likewise, the Church of God has been known historically as a preaching church. When recounting the phenomenal growth that occurred in 1910, the late Dr. Charles W. Conn said:

> *"During the year, the ministers preached everywhere they could gain an audience—in churches, under tents, in open fields, under brush arbors, in homes, in schoolhouses, on street corners, or to individuals met by chance. They preached because of an inner compulsion known as a divine calling; they preached because the message of God was burning upon their hearts; they preached because they loved their fellowman; they preached because they must preach or go to hell. They preached because there were sinners to rescue, believers to baptize, afflicted to heal, skeptics to*

convince, minds to train, and hopeless ones to comfort. They received no praise and did not expect it; they did not preach for plaudits of men or because of vanity of heart—they preached because they had to preach. The choice was God's, and the responsibility was theirs. They were sometimes stoned, pelted with rotten eggs and tomatoes, ridiculed, scorned, cursed, reviled, maligned, beaten, spat upon, shot at, feared, and sometimes loved; but they were not ignored ... They received little or no pay; for five out of six worked during the day and preached at night. But they still preached ... and as they preached, many heard and believed, and the Pentecostal faith spread wonderfully."

Preaching is rooted in Scripture and revealed in the unfolding story of the church. Preaching did not emerge from empirical research or the church's experimentation with various communication techniques. The church does not preach because preaching is thought to be a good idea or an effective communication technique. Rather, we preach because we have been commanded to preach.

The Context of Our Preaching

The world to which we are being sent is a world that is ever-changing and becoming increasingly complex. Political alliances are constantly in a state of flux. We continually hear threats of nuclear and biological terrorism and weapons of mass destruction. Violence is an epidemic. Monetarily, a downturn in the global economy can devastate a nation overnight. Social norms once taken for granted are publicly ridiculed, and society has deteriorated to the point that, in the words of Jeremiah, *"we have forgotten how to blush"* (see Jeremiah 6:15; 8:12). It is an era fraught with paradigm shifts, geopolitical changes, and environmental concerns. The

Pastor Dr. Claudine Benjamin

world longs for men and women who will effectively address the multitude of political and societal ills, but instead of statesmen, it gets politicians.

Gone are the days of the enlightenment. Enter a world that has embraced secular humanism and moral relativism, and denies the existence of absolute truth. Multiple plausibility structures are continually constructed, and the impossibility of objective interpretation is continually invoked. Power has shied to those who control information. Truth has been regulated to technology, and beauty has been subjected to the eye of the beholder. Feelings have become synonymous with being. Philosophy has shied to the existential. Education has shied to the skeptical. The arts have shied to the sensual. Men have shied to the transcendental, believing that they are their own gods and do not have a need for redemption.

Ours is a world that lives in fear. We see a rising debt and a fragile economy, and we worry. We see a rising crime rate and rampant lawlessness, and we worry. We see a drug crisis, an AIDS epidemic, and degenerating moral values, and we worry. We see the secularization of society, racial divisions, homelessness, physical and sexual abuse, and we worry. We see the systematic self-destruction of the family unit, and we worry. Perhaps, the questions that continue to clamor for an answer are these: Is anybody listening? Does anybody really care?

One of the most celebrated and best-loved preachers in our day is Billy Graham. As of April 25, 2010, when he met with Barack Obama, Dr. Graham has been a spiritual advisor to twelve United States Presidents and is number seven on Gallup's list of admired people for the twentieth century. It is said that Graham has preached in person to more people around the world than any other preacher

The Urgency in Winning Souls

in history. According to his staff, as of 1993, more than 2.5 million people had *"stepped forward at his crusades to accept Jesus Christ as their personal Savior."* Behind Billy Graham's messages are five assumptions. He writes:

> *When I go out and proclaim the Gospel, in every congregation and in any group—whether it is on a street corner in Nairobi; or in a meeting in Seoul, Korea; or in a tribal situation in Zaire; or in a stadium in New York City—I know there are certain things that are true in the hearts and minds of all people...First, life's needs are not met by social improvement or material affluence. This is true around the world and in every culture. Jesus said, "A man's life does not consist in the abundance of his possessions" (see Luke 12:15). Second, there is an essential emptiness in every life without Christ. All humanity keeps crying for something, something—they do not know what it is. Give a person a million dollars—it doesn't satisfy. Or give him sex and every form of sensuality; that too never satisfies the deep longing that keeps crying for satisfaction...These past two years I have spoken at a number of the world's most famous universities, and I have heard the pitiful cry of youth who are intellectually, psychologically, and spiritually lost. Pascal was right when he said, "There is a God-shaped vacuum in every life that only God can fill." When we proclaim the Gospel, we're talking directly to that emptiness. Next, we can assume in our hearers loneliness. Some have called it "cosmic loneliness"... it is everywhere: loneliness in the suburbs, loneliness in the ghettos, loneliness in Africa, loneliness in Latin America, loneliness in Japan. It is a loneliness that only God can fill. Fourth, we*

are speaking to people who have a sense of guilt. This is perhaps the most universal of all human experiences, as it is devastating...That is what the cross is all about. When we preach Christ, we are speaking directly to the nagging, depressing problem of guilt.

Fifth, there is the universal fear of death. We do not like to talk about death in our generation. But death is real. The subtle fear cannot be silenced. But here is the good news: our Lord came to nullify death. In His own death and resurrection, He made three things inoperative: sin, death and hell. That's the message of the cross! It is for a time such as this and to a world such as ours that you and I have been called to stand and announce, "The Spirit of the Lord is upon me, because he hath anointed me to preach the gospel to the poor; he hath sent me to heal the brokenhearted, to preach deliverance to the captives, and recovering of sight to the blind, to set at liberty them that are bruised, to preach the acceptable year of the Lord." (Luke 4:18-19 - KJV). The gospel is the panacea for the world's ills and the solution for man's sin. As cool water is to a thirsty soul, the gospel gives "good news from a far country" (see Proverbs 25:25).

The word *gospel*, euangelion, is an all-encompassing term used to describe the "good news" that God has made salvation available to fallen man through His Son, Jesus Christ. This salvation was promised beforehand through the prophets and accomplished in the coming of the Messiah into the world (see Romans 1:2-4). It is described in the King James Version as "the gospel of God" (see Romans 1:1), "the gospel of His Son" (see Romans 1:9), "the gospel of Christ" (see Romans 1:16), "the gospel of the Kingdom" (see Matthew 4:23), "the gospel of the grace of God" (see Acts 20:24), "the gospel of salvation" (see Ephesians 1:13), "the gospel of peace" (see Ephesians 6:15), and "an everlasting gospel" (see Revelation 14:6). While all of these modifiers reveal distinctive aspects of the message, the gospel is one central truth: *"Christ Jesus came into the world to save sinners, among whom I am foremost of all" (1 Timothy 1:15).*

The mission of the Church of God is to communicate the full gospel of Jesus Christ in the Spirit and power of Pentecost. The term "full gospel" encompasses salvation (see Romans 1:16-17), justification by faith (see Romans 3–5), sanctification by the Spirit (see Romans 6–8), baptism in the Holy Spirit (see Acts 1: 4-5; 2:38-39), fruit and gifts of the Spirit (see Galatians 5:22-23; 1 Corinthians 12–14), and healing and deliverance (see Mark 16:17-18). It is the proclamation that Jesus is Savior, Sanctifier, Baptizer, Healer, and coming King! It is all about Jesus. If the context of our preaching is "the world," the content of our preaching must be "the gospel."

In the words of the apostle Paul: *"For Christ did not send me to baptize, but to preach the gospel, not in cleverness of speech, so that the cross of Christ would not be made void. For the word of the cross is foolishness to those who are perishing, but to us who are being saved it is the power God. For since in the wisdom of God the world through its wisdom did not come to know God, God was well-pleased through the foolishness of the message preached to save those who believe." (1 Corinthians 1:17-18, 21).*

The words above were addressed to the church in the city of Corinth, one of the largest cities in the Roman Empire. Located on a large isthmus about fifty miles west of Athens, this cosmopolitan Greek city was on a major trade route and had a thriving economy.

Pastor Dr. Claudine Benjamin

Greeks, Romans, Jews, and a mixed multitude of sailors and merchants flocked to this crossroads. The Isthmian athletic games were held biennially there. By the end of the second century, Corinth had become one of the richest cities in the world. Paul believed Corinth was a strategic city of influence, but it was full of sin. It was one of the most wicked cities of ancient times. Degradation, immorality, and heathen customs abounded.

If you wanted to condemn someone as an immoral person, you would call him a "Corinthian." Before Paul's ministry, not a single Christian was known to reside in Corinth. In recalling his outreach to the city, he wrote: *"And when I came to you, brothers and sisters, I did not come as someone superior in speaking ability or wisdom, as I proclaimed to you the testimony of God. For I determined to know nothing among you except Jesus Christ, and Him crucified. I also was with you in weakness and fear, and in great trembling, and my message and my preaching were not in persuasive words of wisdom, but in demonstration of the Spirit and of power, so that your faith would not rest on the wisdom of mankind, but on the power of God." (1 Corinthians 2:1-5).* Summarizing the content of his preaching, Paul said: *"Now I make known to you, brothers and sisters, the gospel which I preached to you, which you also received, in which you also stand, by which you also are saved, if you hold firmly to the word which I preached to you, unless you believed in vain. For I handed down to you as of first importance what I also received, that Christ died for our sins according to the Scriptures, and that He was buried, and that He was raised on the third day according to the Scriptures." (1 Corinthians 15:1-4).*

The apostle Paul believed that the simple message of the death, burial, and resurrection of Jesus Christ had a "built-in" power to deliver men and women from the domain of darkness and translate them into the kingdom of light. The Holy Spirit, Paul believed, takes the message preached, communicates it to the heart and mind with power, and breaks down every barrier. The gospel is the power of God unto salvation (see Romans 1:16). Charles Spurgeon, in the book, Lectures to My Students, he advised:

> *Regardless of the text you take, make a beeline to the cross. For the cross is the strength of any minister, and I would not be without it for the world. A preacher without the cross is like a soldier without his weapons or a laborer without his tools. Without the cross, I would be like a pilot without a compass or an artist without a brush. Let others preach of the joys of heaven and the terrors of hell. Let others preach of the sacrament and thereby the church. Let others preach of social reform and social issues. But give me the cross. Let me preach the cross. For the cross is the only instrument that has ever turned the world upside down and caused men to forsake their sins.*

The Construction of Our Preaching

Biblical preaching begins with the preparation of the messenger. E.M. Bounds said, *"Preaching is not the performance of an hour. It is the outflow of a life."* It is the overflow of the heart that gives the lips full speech. Communion with God in prayer and consistent Bible study is not only elemental for effective preaching but also absolutely essential for a productive life. When Jesus called His disciples, He did so *"that they might be with Him and that He might send them out to preach" (Mark 3:14)*. The implication is that "being with Him" was a prerequisite for preaching "for Him." Ministry originates and flows out of fellowship with Him. The apostle Paul urged Timothy to study (see 2 Timothy 2:15), make prayer a priority (see 1 Timothy 2:1), and then he demonstrated this precept by his own example. He said the hard-working farmer must be the first to partake of the crops (see 2 Timothy 2:6) and warned of the possibility of preaching to others and yet finding oneself disqualified from the race (see 1 Corinthians 9:27).

The importance of devotion cannot be overemphasized. The richer your devotion, the richer your sermons will be. However, a warning must be given at this point: Be careful of using prayer and Bible study as a means to an end. Far too many ministers have succumbed to the trap of using devotional time for "text hunting" or "sermon hunting." Spending time with Jesus is not a means to an end. He is the end. Inevitably, however, as you spend time in His presence, the Holy Spirit will illuminate and apply the Word of God to your life. He will give you insight into Scripture or burden you with a particular need in your life or your congregation. Practice the discipline of journaling your thoughts and the words God speaks to you. These reflections will be invaluable to your sermon preparation and help chronicle your own spiritual journey. When it comes to message preparation:

1. **Determine the need.** Sermon construction begins with discernment. *"What is the need?"* Is there a need for salvation? For healing? For correction? For encouragement? For Spirit baptism? For Christian growth? What is God doing? What is He saying? Needs are usually discerned in times of prayer, Scripture reading, fasting, and/or simply living with those whom the Lord has called you to shepherd.

2. **Select the appropriate scripture.** Sometimes, the scripture will be an entire book of the Bible, or other times, it will be

a lengthy passage containing a story or teaching. It may be a character study or, at times, one verse of Scripture.

3. **Gain an understanding of the text.** Properly interpret the selected passage of Scripture. To do so, read it in its immediate context and in the larger context of the entire chapter and book. If there are parallel passages, consult those. A Bible dictionary, concordance, and books devoted to word studies can help clarify the meaning of each word. A Bible encyclopedia helps gain a broad understanding of the cultural settings, ceremonies, or historical subjects mentioned in the passage.

4. **Outline the passage.** The outline will usually follow the order of the text and initially contain the actual wording of the verses. Many times, a pattern will emerge, and with the help of a dictionary and thesaurus, contemporary words or phrases can be used to identify each point.

5. **Consult commentaries and other authors.** It is important to know how this text or verse has been treated historically. Commentaries and theological textbooks provide a ready reference for any doctrine that might arise or be impacted by the text.

6. **Develop the message.** Identify the text, interpret the text, and surrender to God in repentance. All too often, we fail to appreciate the gravity of such a moment and simply tack on an invitation at the conclusion of our sermons without any real plan or forethought on how we will end the message to call for a decision. There is seldom a flow from the sermon

to the appeal. Many times, it comes across as an addendum, an appendage to the proclamation rather than the goal of proclamation. Worse yet is the manner in which we extend the invitation. The directions are often indefinite, and what is being called for is unclear. Often, the tone is, *"If there is anyone here who would like to receive Jesus as their Savior,"* rather than, *"those of you here who want to accept Jesus as your Savior, come forward."* Ministers all too often preach past the point of conviction and miss the climax of the service when souls are ready to be gathered in, appearing to be more concerned about reaching the conclusion of their sermon than casting the net and calling for conversion. It is my opinion that the aim of every service ought to be the invitation. The purpose of preaching is to bring men to Christ, and once the message has been communicated, whether or not you have reached your conclusion, it is time to call for a verdict. As one of my preaching mentors is fond of saying, *"Go to the pulpit looking toward the altar."*

8. **Deliver from the heart.** Whether you preach from a manuscript, outline, or speak extemporaneously, deliver it with conviction. David Hume was a skeptic and condemned much of what the Christians held dear. One day, as he was rushing through the streets of his city, hurriedly putting on his raincoat, someone stopped him and said, *"Mr. Hume, where are you going in such a hurry?"*

"To hear George Whitfield," came the answer.

Utterly surprised, the questioner asked, *"Why, you don't believe what Mr. Whitfield does, do you?"*

"Certainly not!" came the answer. *"But Whitfield does, and I want to hear a man who does."*

The Call for Biblical Preaching

The Great Commission depends on giving faithful witness to God's saving work through Jesus Christ. Whoever calls on the name of the Lord will be saved, but how will they hear and believe on Him without a preacher? Never has there been a greater need for a preacher and the preached Word of God than there is today. The call to preach is not occasioned by heredity, achieved by the developing oratorical skills, nor conveyed by the hands of the presbytery. The call to preach is born in the heart of God and communicated by the agency of the Holy Spirit. Often, this call predates one's birth.

The Word of the Lord came to Jeremiah and said that he had been sanctified and ordained to be a prophet from his mother's womb (see Jeremiah 1:5). The same was true for Isaiah who said, *"The Lord called me from the womb"* (see Isaiah 49:1). The apostle Paul said that it was God who separated him from his mother's womb, and called him by His grace for the purpose of revealing His Son in him that he might preach among the Gentiles (see Galatians 1:15). Scripture is replete with biographical data of preachers and prophets and how they came to discover God's sovereign call. Samuel awakened to his call when he learned to distinguish between the voice of God and that of Eli. Moses heard his during a crisis encounter with God late in life while standing barefoot before a burning bush on Mount Horeb. For Isaiah, his call came through a divine revelation of the Lord of hosts in the temple the very year that King Uzziah died.

Pastor Dr. Claudine Benjamin

Paul had an encounter with the resurrected Lord while journeying on a road to Damascus. Each was unique, but all were divine and directional. And so it is today. God still calls men and women to the sacred service of delivering His Word. It comes in various forms and under differing circumstances; nevertheless, His call is certain and definite. It is often described as an inescapable, irresistible inner compulsion, a sense of absolute urgency to preach the gospel of Jesus Christ. Often, this constraint is accompanied by a sense of burden, which is evidenced by fruit. But to those who accept His call, God promises His timeless presence.

David Livingstone was born in Blantyre, Scotland, in 1813. As a young lad, many times he would sit on his father's knee and listen to stories of great missionary exploits being told to him. His young heart was constantly stirred, and he prayed that the day would come when he would serve the Lord in such a fashion. A turning point came when his heart was challenged by the reading of the life of Karl Gutzlaff, the Austrian medical missionary. One day he got down on his knees and prayed this prayer, *"Send me anywhere, only go with me. Lay any burden on me, only sustain me. Sever any ties but the ties that bind me to Your service and to Your heart."* And, he said that through it all, the words of the Lord came to him, *"Lo, I am with you always, even to the end of the age" (Matthew 28:20 - NKJV).* He married Mary, a choice young woman, daughter of the famous missionary Robert Moffat, and set out to serve in Africa. Upon arrival in his place of ministry, he noted in his diary, *"The haunting specter of the smoke of a thousand villages in the morning sun has burned in my heart."* He moved ever northward into unknown territory. Then he sent his wife and family back home. The next time he met Mary was five years later. When she saw him, she did not recognize him. His face had been burned to a crisp and black, having a leather-like appearance from having lived through the ravages of climate and disease. He had been attacked by a lion that had torn one of his shoulders completely apart. He had walked into the branch of a tree that had totally blinded one eye and damaged the other. Yet, every time he walked through the halls of universities to lecture, thousands would stand to their feet in applause, recognizing that a giant among men was among them. After his return to Africa, he continued his work. During his long, arduous career, he was separated for long spans of time from the ones he loved. Then, after he and his wife were reunited, she became critically ill and died shortly thereafter. Kneeling beside her grave, he wept and said, *"My Jesus, my King, my Life, my All, I again commit my life to thee. I shall place no value on anything I possess or in anything I do, except in relation to Thy kingdom and to Thy service."* And through it all, the words of the Lord came to him again, *"Lo, I am with you always, even to the end of the age."*

In 1873, David Livingstone died on his knees in a village in the heart of Africa. In the words of Ravi Zacharias, *"Here is the quality of the life of a man who highlights for us the power that comes from being in touch with the world, from being in touch with his message, and being out of touch with his own comforts and his own rights."* Having lived that quality of life, he left an ineradicable memory of Christ in the heart of the African people. And so it is, in preaching amid those who bow their knees to other gods, you and I, in touch with them, in touch with God, and out of touch with our own comforts, can reach the masses for Christ.

Mark L. Williams, D.Min. | D.D.

Assistant General Overseer
Executive Director, Division of Education

Chapter 20

Personal Evangelism and the Great Commission

The *Personal* Great Commission

D. T. Niles once said, *"Evangelism is one beggar telling another beggar where to find bread."* This statement captures the personal nature of evangelism, but what about the *great* in the Great Commission? The juxtaposition of these two words—*personal* and *great*—warrants deeper reflection.

When we think of the Great Commission, we envision a global movement—the church advancing the gospel across nations. We picture believers from every corner of the world preaching Christ to the lost. But how does this mission become personal? Where does the individual disciple fit within God's plan for the worldwide proclamation of salvation?

The answer is best illustrated in Scripture through the account of Jesus healing the demon-possessed man of Gadara, recorded in Mark 5:1–20.

Pastor Dr. Claudine Benjamin

Most of Jesus' ministry took place in and around Capernaum, a city on the northwestern shore of the Sea of Galilee. This freshwater lake, which feeds into the Jordan River, bordered both Jewish and Gentile regions. The western shore belonged to Galilee, a Jewish province, while the eastern side was home to Gentiles. Southeast of the lake and east of the Jordan River lay the Decapolis—a Greek term meaning *Ten Cities*. Among these cities were Gerasa, Gergesa, and Gadara, and their inhabitants were often referred to as Gerasenes, Gergesenes, or Gadarenes. This region lay beyond Israel's borders, where people did not worship the God of Abraham, Isaac, and Jacob.

It was in this pagan land that Jesus encountered one of the most tragic figures in scripture—a man possessed by demons. Known as *Legion*, he was out of control, living among the dead in a state of isolation and torment. Others had tried to help him, but his inner bondage was stronger than human intervention. No earthly power could change him—only Jesus Christ, the Son of God. And when Christ commanded the demons to leave, the man was completely delivered, transformed, and restored.

What happened next demonstrates how personal evangelism connects with the Great Commission: *"And when He got into the boat, he who had been demon-possessed begged Him that he might be with Him. However, Jesus did not permit him, but said to him, "Go home to your friends, and tell them what great things the Lord has done for you, and how He has had compassion on you." And he departed and began to proclaim in Decapolis all that Jesus had done for him; and all marveled." (Mark 5:18–20 - NKJV).*

The man longed to follow Jesus. Given his dramatic transformation, it seemed only logical—perhaps even strategic—for him to travel

The Urgency in Winning Souls

with Christ and share his testimony. He could have been a powerful witness, a living example of Jesus' authority over demonic forces, drawing great crowds to hear the gospel. Yet, Jesus did not permit him to join the traveling disciples. Instead, He commissioned him to go home and testify to those who knew him best. Why? Because evangelism begins at home. Before reaching the nations, the gospel must transform households, communities, and friendships. Jesus saw the greater need—not just one man's devotion but an entire region's salvation.

The man obeyed without hesitation. He returned home and began to proclaim the good news, sharing his testimony with those who had once feared or pitied him. His credibility was undeniable; the people had witnessed his past torment and now beheld his miraculous transformation. Even the local farmers confirmed his deliverance, making his testimony all the more powerful.

His faithfulness bore fruit. In Mark 7:31, Jesus returned to Decapolis, the very region where He had sent the man to witness. By then, the impact of his testimony was evident. Crowds flocked to Jesus, leading to remarkable miracles, including the healing of a deaf man (see Mark 7:33–37) and the feeding of four thousand people (see Mark 8:1–9). What drew so many to Jesus? Perhaps it was the bold witness of one man who obeyed the Lord's command.

This account exemplifies how the Great Commission is fulfilled on a personal level. God does not call every believer to a public platform, but He calls each one to share the gospel within their sphere of influence. If you are saved, you have a testimony—a story of transformation through Christ. Like the healed man of Gadara,

Pastor Dr. Claudine Benjamin

you are called to proclaim the great things the Lord has done for you. Who in your life needs to hear the good news today?

Chapter 21

Reaching Unreached People: World Missions and the Great Commission

World Missions is not merely an aspect of the church's work—it is **the very heartbeat of the Great Commission**. The mission of God is woven into the fabric of scripture, from Genesis to Revelation. Jesus Christ did not come only for a select group of people; He came **for all nations, all tribes, and all tongues**. His sacrifice on the cross was the ultimate expression of God's love for the world (John 3:16), and His command to His followers was clear: *"Go ye therefore, and teach all nations, baptizing them in the name of the Father, and of the Son, and of the Holy Ghost: Teaching them to observe all things whatsoever I have commanded you: and, lo, I am with you always, even unto the end of the world. Amen."* (Matthew 28:19-20)

Despite the clarity of this mandate, many churches today treat missions as a secondary endeavor—one program among many. But World Missions is not a department; it is the very reason the church exists. Without evangelism, the church loses its purpose and disobeys its calling.

Pastor Dr. Claudine Benjamin

Dick Hillis rightly stated: *"It is not our responsibility to bring the world to Christ; but it is our responsibility to take Christ to the world."*

This distinction is vital. We cannot force anyone to accept salvation, but we **must** ensure that every person has the opportunity to hear the message of Christ. The church exists for three primary reasons:

1. **Ministry to the Lord**—Worship, prayer, and glorifying God.
2. **Ministry to the Body**—Strengthening believers through discipleship and care.
3. **Ministry to the World**—Evangelism, missions, and acts of service.

Undergirding each of these is **love**, for love is the defining mark of a true Christian (see John 13:35). The greatest love ever demonstrated was God's love in sending His Son (see Romans 5:8). As His disciples, we are called to follow His example by carrying His message to those who have never heard.

The Biblical Foundation of Missions

Though the words *mission* and *missionary* are not explicitly found in scripture, the concept is deeply embedded in God's redemptive plan. The **entire Bible is a missionary book**—from God calling Abraham to bless the nations (see Genesis 12:1-3) to the final scene in Revelation, where people from **every tribe, language, and nation** stand before God's throne (see Revelation 7:9).

The word *missionary* comes from the Latin *missio*, meaning "to send," which parallels the Greek *apostello*, meaning "the sent ones." A missionary is not merely one who **goes**; he is one who is **sent**—commissioned by God and the local church to proclaim the gospel (see Acts 13:1-3).

Yet, missions is not simply about evangelizing; it is about **making disciples**. Jesus commanded that we **baptize** and **teach**, ensuring that new believers grow in faith and maturity. This is why mission work is incomplete without **church planting**. A true missionary effort establishes a self-sustaining body of believers who continue the work of the gospel in their own culture.

The Role of the Church in Missions

Every local church plays a role in fulfilling the Great Commission. The pastor is the local leader of this divine mission. If a pastor does not believe in or emphasize missions, the congregation will likely not prioritize it either. Where there is **silence in the pulpit about missions, there will be silence in the pews**.

World Missions is not an optional endeavor—it is a command from Christ Himself. Every believer must recognize their personal responsibility to participate in spreading the gospel.

The Great Commission: A Divine Assignment

The word *commission* means **an authoritative command, a charge, and a power of authority given for a specific purpose**.[2] The Great Commission is not just a suggestion—it is an assignment from Jesus Christ to His followers.

---

[2] Random House Unabridged Dictionary (New York: Random House, 1999), 412.

Key Great Commission Passages

Throughout Scripture, Christ issued His final command in various ways, reinforcing the call to missions.

1. **Matthew 28:18-20 – The Command to Make Disciples**

This passage is perhaps the most well-known statement of the Great Commission. Jesus declared: *"...All power is given unto me in heaven and in earth. Go ye therefore, and teach all nations, baptizing them in the name of the Father, and of the Son, and of the Holy Ghost: Teaching them to observe all things whatsoever I have commanded you: and, lo, I am with you always, even unto the end of the world. Amen."*

Three key elements stand out:

1. **Power**—Jesus assures us that we do not fulfill this mission in our own strength. His power and authority equip us.
2. **Purpose**—The call is to **make disciples, baptize new believers, and teach them** the Word of God.
3. **Presence**—Jesus promises to be with us as we obey His command.

True discipleship requires commitment. In biblical times, disciples followed their rabbis so closely that they were said to be **"covered in the dust of their feet."** This reflected their total devotion to learning and living out their teacher's ways. Today, Christ calls His followers to the same level of commitment.

2. Mark 16:15-18 – The Urgency of the Mission

Jesus also commanded: *"...Go ye into all the world, and preach the gospel to every creature. He that believeth and is baptized shall be saved; but he that believeth not shall be damned. And these signs shall follow them that believe; In my name shall they cast out devils; they shall speak with new tongues; They shall take up serpents; and if they drink any deadly thing, it shall not hurt them; they shall lay hands on the sick, and they shall recover."*

This passage underscores three crucial aspects:

1. **The Call to Go**—Every nation, every people group, and every individual must hear the gospel.
2. **The Consequence of Rejection**—Those who reject Christ will face eternal separation from God.
3. **The Power of the Believer**—Signs and wonders will follow those who go in obedience to Christ's command.

3. Luke 24:47-48 – The Call to Preach Repentance

Jesus declared: *"...repentance and remission of sins should be preached in his name among all nations, beginning at Jerusalem. And ye are witnesses of these things."*

Repentance involves:

1. **Godly sorrow** for sin.
2. **Confession** of wrongdoing.
3. **A decision to turn away** from sin.
4. **Restitution** where possible.

5. **Receiving forgiveness.**

This message is to be proclaimed to **all nations**. No one is exempt from the call to salvation.

The Core Values of World Missions

James condemns churches that prioritize wealth and luxury over **practical Christian service**. True mission work focuses on four core values:

- **Winning the lost**—Sharing the gospel with those who have never heard.
- **Discipling believers**—Ensuring spiritual maturity in new converts.
- **Training leaders**—Raising up pastors, missionaries, and workers.
- **Caring for the needy**—Serving the poor, homeless, and destitute.

Missions is not a program—it is **the purpose of the church**. Since the heart of God beats for the lost, all who follow Him must share in this mission.

"If a Christian is not involved in missions, he or she is not doing His will."

The Call That Cannot Wait

As we come to the close of this book, the message remains clear and resounding: the time is short, the harvest is ripe, and the laborers are few. The urgency of winning souls is not just a

The Urgency in Winning Souls

passionate plea but a divine mandate given to every believer by our Lord Jesus Christ. The Great Commission is not an option for the church; it is the very heartbeat of our faith and the purpose for our existence.

In a world growing darker by the day, the light of the gospel must shine brighter through us. Souls are hanging in the balance—some who may never hear the truth unless we speak, go, give, and pray. Heaven is real. Hell is real. Eternity is certain. And love must compel us to act.

Let us rise up as ambassadors of Christ, clothed in compassion, driven by truth, and empowered by the Holy Spirit. Let us no longer be silent or distracted but urgent, intentional, and obedient. This is our moment in history. Let us not waste it.

May our hearts burn with the fire of evangelism. May our feet be swift to carry the good news. And may our lives be fully surrendered to the mission of making disciples of all nations—starting with the one soul right in front of us.

The Great Commission is still great.

The time is now.

The call is yours.

Go.

"And he said unto them, Go ye into all the world, and preach the gospel to every creature." (Mark 16:15).

Pastor Dr. Claudine Benjamin

"Some wish to live within the sound of church or chapel bell; I want to run a rescue shop within a yard of hell." —C.T.

Chapter 22

Equipping the Church for Evangelism

In a world growing increasingly dark and distant from God, the church must arise—not merely as a place of worship but as a training ground for battle. The call to evangelism is not an extracurricular activity in the life of the believer—it is the heartbeat of the Christian life. Evangelism is the church's divine assignment and its most urgent mission.

To reach the lost, the church must be equipped. A church that is untrained is a church that is unprepared. A church that is unprepared will be ineffective. The time is now to equip every believer to become a soul-winner, an ambassador of Christ, and a light in the darkness.

The Church: God's Strategic Instrument

God's strategy to reach the world has always included His people. From the prophets of old to the apostles in the New Testament, God has consistently used men and women to deliver His message. Today, He continues to use the church as His instrument for salvation on earth.

Pastor Dr. Claudine Benjamin

In Ephesians 4:11-12, Paul writes: *"And he gave some, apostles; and some, prophets; and some, evangelists; and some, pastors and teachers; for the perfecting of the saints, for the work of the ministry, for the edifying of the body of Christ."*

This scripture makes it clear: leaders in the church are not just called to preach but to equip. Their role is to train, mentor, and mobilize the saints for the work of the ministry—which includes evangelism.

Barriers to Evangelism in the Church

Before we can effectively equip, we must acknowledge and confront the barriers that hinder evangelism in many congregations:

1. Fear of Rejection or Failure

Many believers worry they won't have the right words or will be rejected. This fear paralyzes them.

2. Lack of Training

Far too many churches do not provide evangelism teaching or opportunities to practice.

3. Complacency and Comfort

In prosperous societies, the urgency of salvation is often lost in the comforts of routine church life.

4. **Unclear Vision**

The people remain inactive without a clear and communicated evangelistic vision from leadership.

These barriers must be addressed through intentional teaching, discipleship, and by creating a church culture where soul-winning is not just celebrated but expected.

Building an Evangelism-Equipping Culture

Equipping the church for evangelism requires a multi-dimensional approach. It involves the mind, spirit, and practical application.

1. **Spiritual Preparation**

Evangelism is not only a task—it is a spiritual mission. Believers must be empowered by the Holy Spirit.

Jesus told His disciples: *"But ye shall receive power, after that the Holy Ghost is come upon you: and ye shall be witnesses unto me..."* *(Acts 1:8a).*

Before any outreach begins, the church must be in prayer. Leaders must foster an atmosphere of spiritual hunger through fasting, intercession, and teaching on the role of the Holy Spirit. Evangelism must flow from spiritual intimacy with God.

2. **Biblical Literacy**

To witness effectively, believers must know what they believe and why. Scripture is our foundation. Equipping should include:

- Key salvation verses (for example, Romans 3:23, 6:23, John 3:16, Romans 10:9-10).

- How to explain sin, repentance, grace, and eternal life.

- Understanding the difference between religion and relationship.

When believers are grounded in the Word, they are not easily shaken or intimidated.

3. Personal Testimony Development

Every believer has a story. One of the most powerful tools for evangelism is the testimony of a changed life. Equip the congregation to share their testimony clearly and concisely, with a focus on what God has done.

Revelation 12:11a says, *"And they overcame him by the blood of the Lamb, and by the word of their testimony..."*

4. Practical Training and Role-play

Workshops, outreach training sessions, and simulated witnessing encounters help believers gain confidence. This is where the theoretical becomes practical. Pair newer believers with seasoned soul-winners. Provide materials such as tracts, gospel cards, and digital tools.

5. Ongoing Discipleship

Evangelism doesn't end at conversion. The church must be ready to disciple new believers. Classes, mentoring programs, and accountability groups are vital for spiritual growth and retention.

Matthew 28:20 instructs us to teach new believers *"to observe all things whatsoever I have commanded you."* Discipleship is the continuation of evangelism.

Leadership: Igniting the Flame

Church leaders must lead by example. When pastors evangelize, the people are inspired to follow. Preaching must include messages that emphasize the urgency of salvation, the reality of eternity, and the joy of bringing others to Christ.

Leaders should:

- Appoint and train an evangelism team.
- Set outreach goals and community engagement plans.
- Create testimony moments during service.
- Celebrate soul-winning victories publicly.

When evangelism becomes part of the church's DNA, growth is inevitable—not only in numbers but in spiritual maturity.

Evangelism as a Lifestyle

The ultimate goal is not just to create evangelism events but to cultivate evangelism as a lifestyle. Every believer must view themselves as a missionary—on their job, in their neighborhood, in their families. The church gathers to be equipped, but it scatters to reach the world.

We must never forget: Heaven and hell are real. Time is short. Jesus is coming soon. The church must be equipped and on fire.

Closing Charge

The hour is late. The harvest is ripe. The laborers are few.

But God is calling His church to rise, to train, to go, and to win.

It is time to equip the church for evangelism—not tomorrow, but today.

"Say not ye, There are yet four months, and then cometh harvest? behold, I say unto you, Lift up your eyes, and look on the fields; for they are white already to harvest." (John 4:35).

Reflection Section

Personal Reflection Questions

1. Are you personally equipped to share the Gospel with someone? If not, what is holding you back?

2. When was the last time you told someone about Jesus?

3. Have you made evangelism a lifestyle, or is it something you occasionally consider?

The Urgency in Winning Souls

4. In what ways can you support or participate in your church's outreach efforts?

5. What spiritual disciplines (prayer, fasting, Bible study) can you strengthen to prepare yourself for soul-winning?

6. Have you shared your testimony recently? How can you better use it to lead someone to Christ?

7. What specific steps can you take this week to reach one lost soul?

Challenge: Choose one person in your life who does not know Jesus. Pray for them daily this week, and look for an opportunity to share the Gospel with them.

Closing Prayer

Father, in the name of Jesus, I thank You for the call to reach the lost. Forgive me for the times I have been silent or hesitant. Stir a holy fire within me to fulfill the Great Commission. Equip me through Your Word, empower me through Your Spirit, and give me boldness to proclaim the Gospel with love and clarity. Use me as Your vessel—within my church, family, community, and beyond. Let me not be content with church as usual, but let my life be a daily mission field. I receive the mantle of a soul-winner, and I say yes to the call. In Jesus' name. Amen.

Scripture Reference List: Equipping the Church for Evangelism

The Great Commission & Evangelism Mandate

- Matthew 28:19–20
- Mark 16:15
- Acts 1:8
- John 4:35

Power of the Holy Spirit

- Luke 24:49
- Acts 2:1–4
- Zechariah 4:6

Equipping the Saints

- Ephesians 4:11–12
- 2 Timothy 2:2
- 2 Timothy 3:16–17

Boldness in Witnessing

- Romans 1:16
- Proverbs 28:1
- Acts 4:29–31

Importance of the Word

- Romans 10:9–10
- Romans 3:23
- Romans 6:23
- John 3:16

Overcoming Fear

- 2 Timothy 1:7
- Isaiah 41:10
- Philippians 4:13

Testimony and Victory

- Revelation 12:11
- Psalm 107:2
- 1 Peter 3:15

Scriptures on Soul Winning and the Great Commission

The Great Commission (The Mandate)

- **Matthew 28:19–20** – Go and make disciples of all nations.
- **Mark 16:15** – Preach the gospel to every creature.

The Urgency of the Harvest

- **John 4:35** – The fields are white already to harvest.
- **Romans 13:11** – Now it is high time to awake out of sleep.
- **Proverbs 24:11** – Deliver those being led to death.

Empowered to Witness

- **Acts 1:8** – You shall receive power to be witnesses.
- **2 Timothy 4:2** – Be instant in season and out of season.
- **Matthew 10:7–8** – As you go, preach, heal, and deliver.

The Reality of Eternity

- **Hebrews 9:27** – It is appointed to man once to die, then judgment.
- **Matthew 25:46** – Everlasting punishment or eternal life.

- **Luke 16:23** – In hell he lifted up his eyes, being in torment.

The Call to Go and Rescue

- **Jude 1:23** – Save others, pulling them out of the fire.
- **Isaiah 6:8** – Whom shall I send? Here am I; send me.
- **Ezekiel 3:18** – Warn the wicked of their ways.

Faithfulness to the Mission

- **1 Corinthians 9:16** – Woe is me if I preach not the gospel.
- **Daniel 12:3** – Those who turn many to righteousness shall shine.
- **Galatians 6:9** – Don't grow weary in well doing.

Prayer of Commitment to the Great Commission

Heavenly Father,

I come before You today with a heart stirred by the urgency of the hour. Thank You for saving me, redeeming me, and calling me into Your Kingdom for such a time as this. I acknowledge that the Great Commission is not a suggestion—it is a command. And I accept that command with humility, responsibility, and a willing heart.

Fill me with boldness, compassion, and the fire of the Holy Spirit to be a soul winner. Open my eyes to the lost around me. Break my heart for what breaks Yours. Let me not be silent while others perish. Give me wisdom to speak, courage to act, and sensitivity to follow Your Spirit's leading.

Whether it is one soul or many, help me to be faithful. Let my life preach louder than my words. Use me in my home, on my job, in my community, and wherever You send me.

Lord, I surrender to the call. I will go. I will speak. I will serve. I will love. Let Your will be done through me.

In Jesus' name.

Amen.

Call to Action: Your Next Steps as a Soul Winner

1. Pray daily for the lost.

Ask God to place specific people on your heart. Write their names down and lift them up in prayer.

2. Prepare your testimony.

Be ready to share what Jesus has done in your life in a simple, honest, and Spirit-led way.

3. Start where you are.

You don't need a microphone or a mission trip to begin. Share the gospel with your family, friends, neighbors, and coworkers.

4. Equip yourself with the Word.

Study key Scriptures on salvation, evangelism, and the power of the gospel. Be ready to give an answer.

5. Partner with your local church.

Get involved in outreach efforts, evangelism teams, or support missions through giving and prayer.

6. Stay filled with the Holy Spirit.

You need divine power, boldness, and discernment. Seek God daily for His guidance and presence.

7. Don't give up.

Not everyone will respond immediately. Keep planting seeds, and trust God for the harvest.

You are called. You are chosen. You are sent.

Go—and win souls for Christ.

Bibliography

Guy P. Duffield and N.M. Van Cleave, Foundations of Pentecostal Theology (Los Angeles: L.I.F.E. Bible College, 1983), 430.

Charles W. Conn, Like a Mighty Army: A History of the Church of God (Cleveland, Tenn.: Pathway Press, 1977), 103-104.

J.D. Douglas, ed., The Work of an Evangelist: International Congress for Itinerant Evangelists, Amsterdam, the Netherlands, (Minneapolis: World Wide Publications, 1984), 96-97.

C.H. Spurgeon, Lectures to My Students (London: Passmore and Alabaster, 1881), I/72.

Max Lucado. Interview. Online: www.preaching.com.

John R.W. Stott, Between Two Worlds (Grand Rapids: Wm. B. Erdmanns Publishing Company, 1994), 92.8 Douglas, Ibid., 107

Marvin J. Newell, *Commissioned* (St. Charles, Illinois: Church Smart Resources, 2010), 44.

www.ingramcontent.com/pod-product-compliance
Lightning Source LLC
Chambersburg PA
CBHW070740160426
43192CB00009B/1516